CHANGED

Doug Bergsma

Changed

Cover by Nick Delliskave
Cover design by Carly Gannon

ISBN-13: 978-1539871736
ISBN: 1539871738

In his new book *Changed*, Doug speaks honestly from his heart and from his own personal experience. This book is about God's miraculous power that is available to change your life. This book speaks intimately and honestly on how to respond to God's dealings and grow in grace on a day-to-day basis. Lastly it shows that God is the God of second chances. He never gives up on us. He is always there patiently waiting for us, and helping us get back up when we fall.

Roger Huang
Founder, San Francisco City Impact

There is no doubt that we relate to people who have been through what we have been through. That is why some people don't like churches and church people. In our effort to be like Christ we come across as "a little better" than those we talk with. Many times, I'm sure it's not intentional, yet it is the persona that exists! I personally have experienced great loneliness and discouragement as a follower of Christ. I have wanted to give up – throw in the towel! Then I am reminded to wait… Jesus changed me. This is not of my own doing. I can't fix anything without His mercy and grace.

My friend, Doug, is about to help you see what Christ can do! Not what a pastor can do, not what a church can do, but what Christ can do with anyone – no matter your life or circumstances! Christianity doesn't mean you get a free pass to a good life. It means you make a good life out of whatever has happened to you. Enjoy being encouraged by Doug as he brings you hope of a great future in Christ! And if you are one who reads the last chapter first – don't do it! Save the best for last… Enjoy!

Dan Seaborn
Founder and President
Winning at Home, Inc.

Doug Bergsma has expertly woven the fundamentals of walking with God into his life story. Throughout his book, *Changed*, you see the development of a relationship with God lived out and processed through real-life situations. The journey involves some humorous encounters and circumstances, while other moments unfold in very sobering difficulties. Each section of the book reveals distinct seasons that one travels through to have intimacy with God. There is also opportunity to self-reflect and invite the Holy Spirit into your own story. Subsequently, you come to understand that life is full of change and choices. Doug simply asks you to consider allowing God into your world to be *Changed*.

Bobby Bogard
Associate Senior Pastor
Gateway Network

By opening his life to us with utter transparency, Doug Bergsma shows us how to experience the transforming, life-altering power of God. *Changed* is a book I highly recommend to everyone, no matter where they are on their spiritual journey. You will find yourself in these pages, and you will discover the path to true, deep, abiding change through Jesus Christ.

Virginia Smith
bestselling author of *The Days of Noah*
and *Just As I Am*

Dedication

I would like to dedicate this book to my lovely wife Caryn for all the endless hours of reflecting and daydreaming she put up with as I put this book together.

Acknowledgments

I would like to give a special thanks to the team who helped me put this book together: Brian Mannor, Judy Schutter, Ginny Smith, Sean Micheal, and my wonderful daughter Carly. You all have been invaluable both in editing, advice and encouragement. Thank you so much for helping make this project possible. I couldn't have got it done without you.

Table of Contents

Foreword

The story of salvation is the greatest story ever told, and it is a story written by God Himself. The power of the Cross and the atoning sacrifice of Jesus that takes a sinner and turns them into a saint is an epic reality that countless millions of us have experienced firsthand. The writer of Hebrews has it right when he calls it *"such a great salvation."*

The book that you hold in your hands is written by a dear friend of mine who, himself, knows what it is to undergo this transformation of grace, this process of *change*. Doug Bergsma is a man who has a story to tell and keen pastoral insight and wisdom into the sometimes difficult to understand journey of faith that we call "salvation."

Changed is an important book, for many reasons. First, it serves as a roadmap for those who have set out on a journey to experience all that Jesus has purchased for us. Wherever you are on this quest, you will find sign posts pointing you forward, with rich insight and intriguing illustrations, bringing the pages of scripture to life and helping make sense of your own story in Christ.

In addition, this book is an answer to many pastors' prayers, because there really are not that many good books to give to new believers that don't feel like dry text books or dumbed down systematic theology. *Changed* will hold your attention, point you towards hope, and give you clear understanding of what God's will is for each one of us.

You can tell a lot about a person by the way they respond in difficult circumstances in life. I have known Doug for many years and watched him walk with great faith and humility in the face of immense pain and challenges. In every case, his resilience and faith in God has inspired me to yield more of *my* life to the changing and maturing power of the Holy Spirit. He is not just a pastor, but an older brother in the faith, whose story and brilliant application of scripture - mixed with personal anecdotes - will produce the "change" that the title implies.

I am grateful that he is willing to share what he has learned along the way and I am confident that the same God who is writing his story will also be the "Author and the Finisher" of all of our faith.

May the Holy Spirit speak to you between every word that you read.

Lee Cummings
Senior Pastor, Radiant Church
Kalamazoo, Michigan

Prologue

Thank you for taking the time to read this book. I'm very excited about it. For those of you who do not know me, I am currently the pastor of a large, vibrant church that is full of life and spiritual energy. In this role, I meet people every day who look up to me as a very spiritual person who somehow materialized before them with a Bible in one hand and a communion cup in the other. They sometimes have a hard time believing that I can truly relate to their problems and struggles. They can hardly imagine the fact that I have ever stood in their shoes, but early on in my life I too was lost and far away from God. I was following my own sinful desires and doing whatever I pleased, which led me in a downward spiral. It took coming to the end of myself to get right with God and begin following His plan for my life.

As I write, I am thinking about four purposes, or four potentially different groups of people who might choose to read this. As a baseline, I want to give a "boots on the ground" picture to anyone who has heard the good news of God's grace and forgiveness but has not yet responded to it. Many questions go through people's minds regarding what it would be like to become a Christian. What could they expect to happen to them? How would it change their life and the way they are currently living? How would it affect their friend-ships, their mindset, their worldview, and their future? As you read on, I will answer these questions using my own life's journey.

The second purpose I have for this book is to provide a true spiritual handbook that will lead you to know God per-sonally and find the exact preplanned pathway that was cre-ated by God specifically for *you* before you were ever born. When we seek to know God in a personal, intimate way there are some things that just need to be in place in our lives. There are some basic things we need to know and understand. Even if we somehow realize this, there are so many conflicting religious philosophies out there. Each one seems to have its own voice with instructions on how to connect with God and how to stay right with God in order to guarantee eternal life. But there is only one pathway to God—only one way to be right with God and find true pur-pose for your life and the hereafter. As I share my transfor-mational spiritual journey, you will see how understanding this affected my life and how it will also affect yours. If you follow the pathway laid out in this book, along with the en-closed arsenal of promises for your life from God's word, you will experience a dramatic change in your life that will affect you and everyone around you for time and eternity.

My third purpose for writing this book is to challenge and motivate those who have walked with God for a long time to never limit what God can do through them. We must never settle or go on cruise control. In the past, I have made some mistakes in this area and have been distracted somewhat from my main mission and purpose. I will share some im-portant things concerning God's dealings with me as my

Heavenly Father that I believe will help you stay on course and develop a new appreciation of our Heavenly Father's intimate involvement in our everyday lives. We must all stay focused and constantly stir ourselves up and aspire to new levels of godliness and fruitfulness in our life's mission. Furthermore, following God's preordained plan for our life is the most exciting way to live. It is my prayer as we journey through these pages together, that we receive fresh inspiration to lay aside every distraction, push past any previous failures, and go all in with God. In Philippians 3:12 -13 (NIV), apostle Paul stated,

> "Not that I have already obtained all this, or have already arrived at my goal, but I press on to take hold of that for which Christ Jesus took hold of me. Brothers and sisters, I do not consider myself yet to have fully taken hold of it. But one thing I do: Forgetting what is behind and straining toward what is ahead."

There is yet a fourth purpose for writing this book. There is one more message about God's incredible grace that I don't want anyone to miss. The last chapter of this book was written by my daughter, Carly. The title of the chapter is *Prodigal Grace*. It eloquently illustrates the truth that no one is beyond the reach of God's forgiveness, and it is never too late to be changed. This message is for those who have fallen and need to get back up. Carly's story will demonstrate to anyone who needs grace that it's already there— no matter what or who they are, or how far they have fallen. Her story will reassure and encourage those who are praying for lost family members to never give up on them.

This book's central message is reflected in the title – *Changed*. By the grace of God, I was changed so I know you can be changed! Through my journey, I learned there is only one way for change to happen and that is through a total rebirth of the human spirit that brings transformation from the inside out.

2 Corinthians 3:18 (KJV) states, "But we all, with open face beholding as in a glass the glory of the Lord, are **changed** into the same image from glory to glory. Even as by the Spirit of the Lord." [emphasis by author].

May God bless you as we journey through the pages of this book together.

Chapter 1
The End of the Road

I climbed the steep embankment along the viaduct and was greeted by the bustling rush-hour traffic on 28th Street. It was hot, humid, and sticky. I hadn't had a shower in days, but at last I was back in familiar surroundings. I stuck out my thumb one last time. I was only three and a half miles from home. One more little burst of energy—one more ride—would bring me to the end of a long and crazy cross-country journey that had taken a number of months. Anxious to keep things moving, I began walking while I hitchhiked. Suddenly, I was eager to get home. After covering about a half mile on foot, I saw a car slow down and pull over into a side parking lot. I dialed up one more burst of energy and ran to it. I threw my duffel bag into the backseat and climbed in. As I settled into yet another unfamiliar seat, I felt very tired, almost exhausted. I hadn't had a good night's sleep for days.

Once my ride dropped me off, I began walking through the neighborhood and up the hill to my house. An old Bible parable about a rebellious prodigal son returning home floated through my head. As I reflected on it, I noted that indeed, I had been that kind of son. I had an overwhelming feeling of identification with the story concerning the son's condition and what he must have felt like coming home.

My mind whirled with all the things I had experienced on my cross-country journey. My friend and I eventually ended up in Denver, Colorado, and found ourselves sleeping in fields and sometimes in car lots under vehicles when it rained. When we ran out of money, we washed dishes and swept bar and restaurant parking lots for food. We met a lady while working for meals and when she discovered that we were living on the street, she offered us a temporary place to stay. As it turned out, this lady was a schoolteacher who supplemented her income by having several boy-friends, or should I say "clients." Interestingly enough, she had two young children. Because of her lifestyle, I think she enjoyed having some extra security around. She assigned me the responsibility to keep the peace if anything got out of hand. As I look back, there were some shaky moments, and I remember sleeping at night with a baseball bat I called "The Equalizer."

As time went on, this new and crazy environment led to parties, drugs, alcohol, and some of the other things you run into in the underbelly of society. My friend and I got a job at Metro Ice Factory in Denver to finance our new lifestyle, but things slowly deteriorated. I had a deep sense of emptiness and a knowing that I had strayed far from the foundations and standards my Christian parents had instilled in me during my childhood. I reflected on the events that finally pushed my life to a tipping point. Smoking pot was the new "in thing" at that time, along with hallucinogenic drugs like LSD, acid, and speed, to name just a few.

I remember one particular time when my friend and I scored some blotter acid that was particularly powerful. As we sat tripped out, listening to blues and psychedelic music, I felt as if I was losing control of my mind. As I stared at my friend across the room, a voice said to me, "Your friend is thinking of killing you. You better kill him before he kills you." The voice was so compelling and powerful that I had an overwhelming urge to follow its suggestion. I summoned all the mental strength I could. I stood up and walked out into the snowy night to get away from the scenario before I did something crazy. The wind was blowing - it was below freezing and snowing hard. All I was wearing was a t-shirt and a pair of jeans, yet I was totally unaware of the cold. I walked to the end of the street. I crossed the normally busy Colfax Avenue in Denver and wandered into a mall parking lot. There was an old couch under the lights at a Salvation Army drop off point, so I sat down on it in the snow and freezing cold, trying to hang onto my mind and survive the ordeal.

That whole evening badly scared me, and it got even worse several days later. I was driving an old car that we had obtained to the store to get some groceries. All of a sudden, I had a drug-induced flashback. I saw myself driving off a cliff. I saw pine trees far below me, and felt the emptiness of space around me. I frantically spun the wheel of the car to avoid driving off the cliff's edge. In actuality, my car spun around in the street, took out a mailbox, and I ended up sitting in someone's yard. Fortunately, I was not hurt, though I was very embarrassed and scared out of my mind. From moment to moment, I began to dread having another flashback. While I was struggling to deal with all of those issues, another event happened shortly after that which pushed me completely over the edge.

From time to time, my friend and I would smoke pot in the restroom of the ice factory where we worked. On one particular day, I got so stoned that my day seemed to be a surreal blur. As I loaded 300-pound blocks of ice into a truck, one of them tipped backwards and fell, crushing the upper part of my finger. Almost instantly, my jersey glove was soaked with blood. I was afraid to take it off. I went straight to the emergency room only to find myself in a waiting room jammed full of battered and hurting people, most of whom had been injured from the previous night's Rolling Stones concert. There I sat with all those depressed people, with my hand wrapped up, feeling the explosive pain that comes with that type of injury. Eventually, it was my turn. The emergency room doctor cut off my glove, revealing a bloody gash that went all the way around my finger above the top joint. The skin wasn't cut, but it was mashed and broken all the way to the bone. The doctor stitched and dressed my finger before putting it in a brace. He sent me home with a prescription for a narcotic-strength painkiller.

Blurry-minded from the painkillers, I got up the next morning and sat out on the deck of the apartment building where we were staying. I looked around at the beautiful view of the mountains of Colorado from the edge of Denver. I looked at the beauty of creation and I contrasted it with my personal world of pain, growing depression, loneliness, and the emptiness in my soul. I tried to drown it all by getting drunk, but that only made things worse. Narcotic painkillers, mixed with alcohol, drove me even further down, and I felt bottomed out—completely at the end of myself, feeling sick and dizzy. I remember saying to myself, "This is it. I've had enough! I'm going home."

Going...Back

The following day, I climbed up onto the interstate in Denver, stuck out my thumb, and headed for home. I got picked up by a van full of hippie freaks who were all smoking pot and listening to blues. I ended up riding with them for hundreds of miles. The van was so full of smoke you couldn't help but be affected by what was going on. They finally dropped me off late at night on the highway, in the middle of nowhere. I remember standing there, stoned out of my mind, feeling very alone.

Not too long after that, an olive-green Barracuda with a 340-six-pack hit the binders and came roaring to a stop in response to my outstretched thumb. Three guys, one with a cowboy hat on, flipped the door open and told me to jump in. The radio was blaring country music. I saw two cases of beer in the backseat and realized that these guys were drunk. I told them, "Hey guys, thanks for the offer, but no thanks." At that point, one of them jumped out and said, "Look, we stopped for you. You need a ride…you better get in." I'm no sissy, but I looked at the 3-to-1 odds on a dark road, along with my need for a ride, and decided to comply. As I climbed in, they shoved a beer into my hand and off we went. We traveled at high speeds for hours through the night, drinking and listening to tunes. That long journey home, along with the mixture of drugs, alcohol, and the contrast of mixed company, gave me a true case of paranoia. I spent hours in fear for my life. I imagined being killed in a fiery car crash and going to hell. I found myself attempting to make deals with God about my life and future if He would just help me survive and get home.

After what seemed to be an eternity, it was all behind me. I was back in familiar surroundings. I walked across my lawn, opened the front door of my house, and stepped inside. I was absolutely exhausted, and it felt so good to be home. My mom and dad were overjoyed to see me back home and in one piece. I knew they had been praying for me night and day. There was no instant communication technology back then, no cell phones for calling and texting. There was no Facebook. If you wanted to call or talk, it took a handful of quarters at a payphone for a two or three-minute call, or you had to write a letter. My parents just had to trust God and pray for me, with very little communication.

The More Things Change...

After arriving back home and resting up, all my old friends started calling me, and a few nights later I found myself at an all-night kegger party at a Lake Michigan cottage with my old friends. The next morning, I returned home, hung over with a headache, feeling empty and lost. It was no different than the way I had felt in Denver before I had left for home. I realized I could not continue to live this way. I just came to the end of myself again. Deep down I had known from a very young age that God loved me and wanted me to serve Him, but I had run away from Him and followed my own pursuits. Doing this had brought me no fulfillment. I was nagged by a constant, underlying fear of getting killed or dying, and frankly, the thought of going to hell forever in payment for my rebellious and sinful lifestyle ruined any opportunity for inner peace.

As I sat alone in the living room, I saw a new, modern Bible translation called *The Living Bible*. I picked it up and opened it up to the inside cover. Unexpectedly, I saw a short note written there from my dad to my mom. It said, "To my wonderful wife on her birthday, given in covenant agreement that our son will turn his life over to the Lord fully and follow Him." Something about that hit me like a ton of bricks. I took the Bible and went soberly up to my bedroom. I held it in my hands and I said, "Lord, I give my life to You totally. I'm done with my old life. I am going to follow You and serve You alone. Please forgive my sins and change my life." Something happened to me at that moment. I felt God's peace settle over me. The kind of peace that only comes when our heart is right with Him. It felt like all the tumblers in my mind and my heart and my spirit came into alignment with God and His plan and purpose for me. I knew right then and there that something old in me had died and was no longer relevant.

The Key to Receiving Grace

As I look back over my life, I realize this was my first true introduction to the grace of God and its amazing power to forgive and bring about a transformation that changes your entire life. Grace is the most amazing essence in the universe. It lets you go free when you don't deserve it. In fact, its very definition is God's undeserved favor. Or to spell it out—**GRACE: G**od's **R**iches **A**t **C**hrist's **E**xpense. Over the years I have heard this popular phrase in sermons and read it in books, but that pretty much wraps it all up. The bottom line of salvation is the fact that Jesus shed His blood on the cross and gave His life to pay for our sins so we wouldn't have to. I knew from a very young age about the story of the cross. With full mental assent, I believed in God and the Bible and in Jesus. I even knew in my heart that it was all true. But it's quite a bit different to know and believe something in your mind versus coming to the point where you realize the way you are living is not right and that something needs to change. When I decided to discard my rebellious and selfish I'll-do-whatever-I-want lifestyle and chose to follow God's will, everything began to change for me. I asked God to forgive me for my past sins and make me a new person on the inside.

The Bible calls this whole process *repentance*. Repentance means to change our mind and go in a different direction. Repentance starts in our hearts. The Holy Spirit brings a deep inner conviction that we are not right with God and an inner knowing that we need to change. As I look back over my life, I realize now that I *knew* who Jesus was, and what He had done for me, but I had never come to a point where I decided I could not do whatever I felt like doing and live any old way I pleased. I just kind of trusted that because I knew who God was and what Jesus had done, I was ok. But I was not ok. I recognized that the path my life had taken was evidence of the downward spiral of someone who hadn't truly decided to change and follow God's will for their life. *Repentance* is the key to making it personal. Repentance is the doorway to a living and working relationship with God.

A great example of repentance is found In the New Testament in the book of Acts. Peter confronted the Jewish nation with their sin of rejecting Christ and crucifying Him. It says that when they heard his words they were cut to the heart, feeling deep inner conviction, and they said, "What should we do to get right with God?" "Peter replied, 'Repent and be baptized, every one of you, in the name of Jesus Christ for the forgiveness of your sins. And you will receive the gift of the Holy Spirit'" (Acts 2:38 NIV). When they did this, three thousand people experienced God's grace of forgiveness and salvation. It was the beginning of The New Testament Church, and today there are nearly two and a half billion living believers in Jesus who have found new life and a new purpose.

When I decided that I was going to follow Jesus and stop doing my life my way, all the lights of grace that bring salvation went on in my heart. Ephesians 2:8-9 (NIV) says, "For it is by grace you have been saved, through faith—and this is not from yourselves, it is the gift of God—not by works, so that no one can boast." Another amazing aspect of experiencing God's saving grace was the fact that the part of me that had formerly been dark and unreceptive to God was now filled with light. I was able to *feel* God's peace, not just know about it in some intellectual way. I could sense His voice speaking to my conscience in a new way that seemed to activate my whole life with new focus and a new desire to please God and do whatever He had called me to do. Before this, it was as if God had been inaccessible. But as a result of grace, I had an amazing, constant, and real sense that I was right with God. It was absolutely amazing. The fear of dying or a dreadful future just disappeared, and an amazing peace took its place instead. My old way of doing life was over, and a new life with a new purpose had begun.

Take Away

It is in our most broken moments that God does some of His best work. The sense of emptiness, loneliness, or the lack of fulfillment that we have all felt at times in our lives can only be rectified by an authentic relationship with Jesus Christ. We can attempt to drown our struggles through substance abuse, work, intimate relationships, and/or countless other offerings of the world, however, they will never do the job that only Jesus can do. In our brokenness, we realize how much we need our Savior, Jesus Christ.

The good news is our salvation is not something that we must earn, but rather, it is freely given through the grace of God. Remember, grace is God's unmerited or undeserved favor. Jesus died on a cross, and His shed blood paid the price for ALL YOUR SINS! Our God transformation begins by believing in who Jesus is, and in what He has done for us. Once we do this, we must make our faith personal by establishing a living and working relationship with God through the act of repenting of our sins (changing our sinful mindset and ridding ourselves of thoughts and actions that separate us from God) and asking for God's forgiveness. Thus begins our lifelong God transformation as we seek to follow God's purposes and will for our lives.

Discussion:

1. When you reflect on the sins and shortcomings of your personal life, do you find it hard to believe that God will freely forgive you of all your sins, regardless of your personal performance? (See what God's word says in *Ephesians* 2:8-9; available below under *Activate Your Faith.*)

2. How have you, now or in the past, tried to drown out your feelings or struggles through distractions like work, intimate relationships, or substance abuse? How did these distractions fail to consistently fulfill your needs?

3. How will beginning a relationship and following Jesus change your thinking and actions through the process of repentance? In other words, how does a life knowing Jesus look different?

4. What was your "tipping point" that brought you to make a personal decision to accept Jesus as your personal Lord and Savior and ultimately choose to follow His will and ways?

Activate Your Faith:

• Watch Pastor Doug's *Exit Strategy*. I pray with you online to personally receive Christ as your Savior and start a new life. Watch online by visiting: www.rockfordres.org/exitstrategy

• Memorize and ponder the following scriptures:

  o *"Very truly I tell you, whoever hears my word and believes him who sent me has eternal life and will not be judged but has crossed over from death to life" (John 5:24 NIV).*

  o *"For it is by grace you have been saved, through faith—and this is not from yourselves, it is the gift of God—not by works, so that no one can boast" (Ephesians 2:8-9 NIV).*

Chapter 2
A New Beginning

"Therefore if any man be in Christ, he is a new creature: old things are passed away; behold, all things are become new." (2 Corinthians 5:17 KJV)

It seemed that overnight everything changed for me. All kinds of things began to happen. First of all, the very next morning I woke up with a clear head. I felt a new sense of security, along with a deep peace in my heart. I also had a new sense of purpose. I simply knew my past was behind me for good. God's forgiveness had wiped my slate clean from guilt. I love the verse in Hebrews 8:12 (NIV) where God says, "For I will forgive their wickedness and will remember their sins no more." It was so amazing not to feel guilty and full of dread about the future. Now, a whole new life had opened up that had been inaccessible to me before. I felt excitement; I knew that I was on the right track. I was now following the path that God had planned for me. It was an amazing mixture of excitement and mysterious wonder. I knew for sure that life was going to be a lot different from here on out.

I began to read the Bible regularly to find out more about God and His will for me, and I finally began to realize what the phrase "to be born again" meant. I had always heard ministers and other Christians quote Bible verses that said if we are to know God, we must be born again. Now that I had experienced the new birth, I actually knew what it meant. My old life had died, and it's like something else inside me had come to life. Suddenly, the doorway opened to a whole new life that had previously been invisible. The light in my spirit turned on, and getting right with God made my new pathway with Him visible and accessible.

As I reflect on this, I think it is so exciting that God preplanned a full life plan for every single one of us— long before He even made the world! Ephesians 1:4 (NIV) says, "For he chose us in him before the creation of the world to be holy and blameless in his sight…" Ephesians 2:10 (KJV) goes on further to say, "For we are his workmanship, created in Christ Jesus unto good works, which God hath before ordained that we should walk in them." To think that God thought of me and came up with a specific plan for me before time began, is flat out amazing. I remember praying, "God, I want to see that life fully. I want to live that life. I want to walk in that plan and do all the good works that You preplanned for me to do."

The Ultimate "How To" Book

After I prayed this prayer, an insatiable hunger for spiritual things flooded my mind and my heart. I came to a new realization that the Bible is a spiritual book with invisible, spiritual power that is activated in our life when we believe what it says and obey it. Something transformational happens in us and through us that is full of divine life and spiritual power. There's no other book like it in the universe. It's alive and is activated by the Spirit of God who lies latently behind the written text. But it is activated only when we believe and obey it.

Here are some of the basic facts:

- The Bible contains 66 books by 40 different authors, written over a long period of time (over twelve hundred years), yet the books flow together cohesively, even though the authors come from all different walks of life, and lived during different periods of time.
- Only the Bible shows how the universe began, who God is, the creation of the world, the origin of sin, the history of man, and even the origins and the names of the nations that we see often in the news headlines today.
- The Bible answers the major questions we want to know about our lives: Where did everything come from? Why am I here? Why is life such a struggle? What is my life's purpose? Where am I going when I die?

[*To find answers for all these questions, including a complete story of where sin originated, how the fallen angel Lucifer became Satan, and how Jesus legally canceled Satan's power on the cross, watch the podcast series...* **The Big Picture** at
http://rockfordres.org/media/sermons/series/the-big-picture/].

Over the centuries, unbelievers and historical revisionists have tried to disprove the Bible and its authenticity; however, archaeological discoveries, science, quantum physics, and competent analysis have systematically continued to shred these contrary arguments and disagreements. One third of the Bible contains predictive prophecy, forecasting historical events that would occur thousands of years later with inerrant accuracy. The Bible is the oldest book in the world, given by divine inspiration, containing an integrated message given from outside of time and showing us the pathway to eternal life. As such, the Bible became the central source of my inspiration. My new life directive. My roadmap. My manual on how to do life God's way.

Lesson #1

As I studied the Bible, one of the first and most important things I discovered was that we must be baptized as a sign that we belong to Christ. Not too long after I turned my life over to Christ, I joined a large group made up of hundreds of young people who had also experienced the grace of God. It was called the "Wealthy Street Community," and we met in downtown Grand Rapids, Michigan. We would get together on Saturday nights with our guitars and Bibles, and worship God while sharing different experiences and things we had learned during the week. Periodically, as many young people turned their lives over to Christ, we would hold baptism services at a local lake. Being baptized is the very first thing that the Bible tells us we must do after we have become a follower of Christ. It symbolizes the fact that we have died to our old way of life, that our sins have been washed away. As we come up out of the water, it symbolizes a brand-new life and a brand-new start.

I remember getting baptized with a number of others on a Saturday night at a boat launch. I had been baptized early on in my life as an infant, in a sprinkling ceremony, but as I studied the Bible, I realized that baptism is something God commands us to do as an act of our will in obedience to

God's word, after we have turned from our sins and become followers of Jesus. As an infant, I had no understanding, no ability to exercise my will to turn from my sins. As nice as many of the baptism and christening ceremonies are, and as good as the motives of many parents and religious leaders are, those types of ceremonies are ineffective and are not a valid representation of what it means to be baptized. Beyond the need to understand what we are taking part in, the sprinkling technique also does not satisfy the idea of complete commitment that true baptism represents. "Baptism" means to be *fully immersed* in water, signifying that our old life is gone, and as we come out of the water, it symbolizes that we have been raised up and cleansed to live a whole new life. Romans 6:1-4 (NLT) says it this way:

"Well then, should we keep on sinning so that God can show us more and more of His wonderful grace? Of course not, since we have died to sin, how can we continue to live in it? Or have you forgotten that when we were joined to Christ Jesus in baptism, we joined him in his death? For we died and were buried with Christ by baptism. And just as Christ was raised from the dead by the glorious power of the Father, now we also may live new lives."

My dad was a well-known pastor in a well-established denominational church. Over the course of his ministry, he often stated his belief in and defense of the validity of infant baptism. On the other side of the house, my mother believed in what the Bible plainly states. I remember listening as they argued and argued about the two different positions. One day, I remember my mom giving my dad a little pamphlet titled, "What the Bible Says About Infant Baptism." My dad, thinking that my mom had finally seen the light on his position, eagerly took the pamphlet and opened it up to read it. To his dismay, it was blank. It said nothing, making the point that I would like to reemphasize. The Bible states nothing at all about infant baptism. Being baptized is something we do after we have changed and decided to follow Christ, and it is very important to do it the way God intended. When we do it His way, it shows our obedience and submission to God and opens the door to the next thing He wants to do in our lives, which is to fill us with His Holy Spirit.

Take Away

When a person chooses to accept and follow Christ, he or she is born again as a new creation in Christ. What does that mean? Your sins have been forgiven, your past has been forgotten, and you have been made brand new! It's as if God pushed the reset button! God shows us that we must get baptized as our very first step as a new believer.

Baptism symbolizes the fact that we have died to our old way of life, and that our sins have been washed away. As we walk out our new life, we have a new and overwhelming sense of purpose. This is because God created each of us with a plan and purpose, a life's mission full of good works that He pre-planned for us long ago. To understand God's plan and His purpose for our lives, we must begin reading His Word (The Bible) that has been divinely written, without error. The Bible should become the central source for your inspiration, life direction, and most importantly, it is literally and spiritually our manual on how to do life God's way.

[For a more in-depth discussion of getting started as a new Christian, see **A Total Makeover** at

http://rockfordres.org/media/sermons/a-total-makeover/

Discussion:

1. Knowing that you are a new creation, have you felt guilt or shame regarding your words, actions, or thoughts from your old life? Why is this wrong thinking?

2. What is the difference between just "reading" God's Word, and believing and obeying what God's Word says?

3. What does your time reading the Bible look like (daily, weekly, or not much at all)? What can you do to become more disciplined in spending time reading God's Word?

4. Why is it important to understand that baptism is an act of obedience that we must choose out of our own free will?

Activate Your Faith:

- If you haven't chosen to get baptized as a sign of obedience to God, find out how you can sign up for baptism in your local church.

- Develop a spiritual discipline by consistently reading God's Word. You can begin by reading a chapter a day starting with the *New Testament* book of *John*, and one chapter each day from the book of *Proverbs.*

- Memorize and ponder the following scripture verses:

   o *"Therefore, there is now no condemnation for those who are in Christ Jesus, because through Christ Jesus the law of the Spirit who gives life has set you free from the law of sin and death"* (Romans 8:1-2 NIV).

   o *"For we are God's handiwork, created in Christ Jesus to do good works, which God prepared in advance for us to do"* (Ephesians 2:10 NIV).

Chapter 3
Spirit Wind

"But you will receive power when the Holy Spirit comes upon you. And you will be my witnesses, telling people about me everywhere..."

(Acts 1:8a NLT)

S hortly after I turned my life over to Jesus, I was introduced to a spiritual experience. In spite of all my religious upbringing I literally knew nothing about this,
even though it is clearly documented in the Bible as a key
ingredient in our lives as believers.

In the fifth book of the New Testament, Acts of the Apostles, there is an amazing story about the wonderful feats and

experiences of Christ's disciples as they shared the good news of salvation and laid the foundation of the early church. Before Jesus ascended to heaven, He told them not to go out and try witnessing for Him right away, but rather to wait for the Holy Spirit to come. The Holy Spirit is the third member of the holy Trinity. His job is to represent and execute the will of God and the divine nature of Jesus on the earth, particularly through the lives of believers. Jesus told His disciples that after His departure they would be filled with the Holy Spirit, and that would give them the ability to be witnesses for Him and live a dynamic life that was filled with power. In Acts 1:8 (NIV) Jesus says, "But you will receive power when the Holy Spirit comes on you, and you will be my witnesses in Jerusalem, and in all Judea and Samaria, and to the ends of the earth." After Jesus ascended to heaven, the disciples of Jesus waited for the Holy Spirit to come. They waited behind closed doors in an upper room partly because they were fearful of persecution by religious leaders, but also in wonderment and expectation of what was coming. Then, early one morning, there came an event that would change human history forever and empower the followers of Jesus in an amazing new manner. Let's read the story from the Word of God exactly as it happened.

> "On the day of Pentecost all the believers were meeting together in one place. Suddenly, there was a sound from heaven like the roaring of a mighty windstorm, and it filled the house where they were sitting. Then, what looked like flames or tongues of fire appeared and settled on each of them. And everyone present was filled with the Holy Spirit and began speaking in other languages, as the Holy Spirit gave them this ability" (Acts 2:1-4 NLT).

Pilgrims from all over the country who were staying in Jerusalem for the Passover Feast, flocked into the streets to hear what all the commotion was about. They *heard* the wind. They *saw* the followers of Jesus praising God in different languages, with tongues of fire on their heads. Some were convinced that what they were witnessing was the results of a wild, drunken party, but the apostle Peter stepped forward and addressed the crowd with a very different explanation. He preached a powerful message to them, telling them that they had made a huge mistake in crucifying Jesus Christ, the very One who had come to save them. But God had overruled it all, and had raised Him from the dead. Now, Jesus had ascended into heaven and sent the Holy Spirit to be an indwelling power for every believer. The Holy Spirit would enable them to be effective witnesses for Him, and show the world who Jesus was.

When all the people heard Peter's message, they were deeply convicted in their hearts that they had made a terrible mistake. They asked Peter, "What should we do to get right with God?" Peter said, in Acts 2:38 (NIV), *"Repent and be baptized every one of you, in the name of Jesus Christ for the forgiveness of your sins. And you will receive the gift of the Holy Spirit."*

This verse lays out the three things that must happen for a person to find eternal life and live a dynamic Christian life the way God intended it to be:

1. Repent and turn from our sins, and decide to accept Jesus as our savior.
2. Be baptized in water as a public sign as we are immersed that our old life is dead. And as we are raised from the water, symbolically represent the new life we are going to live.
3. Be filled with the Holy Spirit, which gives us the power to live an effective Christian life.

Following the Wind

As I reflect back over my life, I can't overemphasize the importance of all three of these things being in place. I remember well the lack of power to witness regarding my newfound faith in my early Christian experience. I specifically recall going out with all my party friends to the local Village Inn pizza parlor. This was the spot where everybody loved to drink and sing beer songs, eat pizza, and just hang out and have a good time. It was a lively, fun place. I used to go there regularly with all my motorcycle buddies and party friends. After high school, I even worked there for a while. Now, shortly after my conversion, I was sitting there with all my friends once again. They were all drinking and hanging out. I tried to tell them what had happened to me. I told them I had asked God to forgive all my sins, and I had given my life to Jesus. Then I told them that I was living a new life and following a new course. They all laughed at me, not in a mocking way, but in utter disbelief. How could this wild party animal, crazy-guy-gone-serious ever get all spiritual and start living with any kind of holy standards at all? That was the question on everyone's mind, to which they quickly assumed, "That's impossible."

I felt weak and incapable of bridging the gap with my friends and helping them make a God connection to the new life I was experiencing. I remember going to the Bible and reading the story about Jesus' disciple Peter who, when Jesus was betrayed by Judas (who was also one of Jesus disciples), denied that he even knew Him. Peter made his denial three times! Jesus had predicted that Peter would get scared and not stand up for his faith. But even though he had been forewarned by Jesus, Peter was weak and incapable, and when he was put to the test he cursed and swore and said he didn't even know who Jesus was. As a result, he was later bitterly sorry and ashamed of himself. Then, in a unique moment that occurred after His resurrection, Jesus forgave and restored Peter. Shortly after that interchange,

Jesus told the disciples that they would get new power to be His witnesses when the Holy Spirit came and filled them.

On the day of Pentecost, the Holy Spirit came and filled all of Jesus' followers with His divine presence and power, enabling them with the special ability to witness and stand up for Him. Peter became a totally different person. The same man who had vehemently denied Jesus three times to save his own skin, stepped forward and put the whole city on trial and accused them of killing Jesus. This brought such deep conviction on them that three thousand people became followers of Jesus in response to Peter's message.

As I read this story, I saw the huge difference in Peter and the way he was before he was filled with the Holy Spirit versus afterwards. The Holy Spirit turned that bumbling, uneducated, bombastic fisherman into a spiritual powerhouse. He was utterly fearless, with a new capability to share his faith. I knew that I needed to be filled with the Holy Spirit. It was God's promise to me.

A New Look

I had been taught a bit differently about the Holy Spirit in the church denomination that I had been raised in. I had been taught that the infilling of the Holy Spirit was not a separate experience from becoming a born again believer. In fact, 1 Corinthians 12:13a (ESV) says that by one spirit are we baptized into the body of Christ. And I must tell you, it takes a revelation of the Holy Spirit in our hearts and minds for us to realize we need salvation. The Holy Spirit enables us to see the light, and it is through His work that we become believers. It is by the Holy Spirit that we have God's divine nature living inside us. But, as I studied the Word of God more closely, I saw that the Bible clearly teaches in multiple places that a special infilling of the Holy Spirit with gifts and power is a separate experience from becoming a born again believer.

Let me give you one example from the book of Acts, chapter 8. One of Jesus' disciples, the evangelist named Philip, went down to Samaria to preach the good news of Jesus. When the people heard his message, they received it with great joy and many were saved, became believers, and were baptized. The news of their conversion came back to Jerusalem, and the apostles realized they needed to do some follow-up work there. So they sent Peter and John down to Samaria. I'll give you the rest of the account straight from Acts 8:14-17 (NLT):

> "When the apostles in Jerusalem heard that the people of Samaria had accepted God's message, they sent Peter and John there. As soon as they arrived, they prayed for these new believers to receive the Holy Spirit. The Holy Spirit had not yet come upon any of them, for they had only been baptized in the name of the Lord Jesus. Then Peter and John laid their hands upon these believers, and they received the Holy Spirit."

This passage, along with others, clearly states that the infilling of the Holy Spirit is separate from the convicting work of the Holy Spirit that initially brings our new birth and salvation. The infilling of the Holy Spirit brings the spiritual aspect of our makeup to its full capacity. We find a deeper connection with God. We find spiritual sensitivity, and special gifts of the Holy Spirit greatly increase our capacity to operate in the spiritual realm, even though we live in a tangible world of time, space, and matter. Some people are afraid of the spiritual aspect of being filled with the Holy Spirit. They think they're going to turn into some kind of flaky, funky person. But that couldn't be farther from the truth. The infilling of the Holy Spirit brings a balance to our lives that was missing before we became believers.

I remember when my new Christian friends prayed for me to be filled with the Holy Spirit. After a worship service, they gathered around me, laid their hands on me, and just asked God to fill me with the Holy Spirit. As I raised my arms in the air and began to ask God to fill me with the Holy Spirit, I became acutely aware of the pack of cigarettes in my front pocket. It felt like that habit was blocking me from fully reaching out to God. Without even opening my eyes, I reached into my pocket and pulled out the pack of cigarettes and threw them behind me, where they scattered all over the floor. It sounds kind of humorous as I look back at it. But sometimes things in our lives that are not right—especially willful, sinful patterns and habits that we have not yet put behind us—can block our ability to receive from God. A moment after I threw those cigarettes behind me, I felt something break loose inside me and I was filled with the Holy Spirit. Almost immediately, as I worshiped God, I received a prayer language in another tongue that I was not familiar with. It was just there. I began to pray fervently in that unknown language (I will talk more about that prayer language later on). As I prayed, I had this inner sense of completion. I knew right then and there that I had everything I needed to go forward in my life's journey.

The Holy Spirit is our inner guide to lead us, day to day, into everything God has for us. One of the main identifying marks of a believer is found in Romans 8:14 (NIV) where it says, "For as many as are led by the Spirit, these are the sons of God."

The Voice of Truth

I remember how different it felt having the Holy Spirit living inside me. It was amazing and revolutionary. Suddenly, someone else was gently guiding my life, instructing me how to live, where to go, what to do or not to do. It was not a dominating, overwhelming force. It was more like a quiet, sure sense of knowing on a much higher level than anything I had ever experienced before. I believe the simplest way to describe it is that I heard God's voice speaking to me through my conscience. When I obeyed that voice, I had an inner sense of peace. I believe that God's peace is the umpire for our souls. Peace is an inner sense that things are right. The Word of God says, "Let the peace of Christ rule in your hearts" (Colossians 3:15 NIV). I think everyone has a conscience and a sense of right and wrong, but when we are apart from God, in spiritual darkness - doing our own thing - we don't have the desire or the power to live by that inner voice. After I asked Jesus into my heart and was filled with the Holy Spirit, it was like the Holy Spirit became intertwined with my spirit and my conscience. My conscience was suddenly razor sharp, because it was one with the Holy Spirit. 1 Corinthians 6:17 (NIV) says, "But whoever is united with the Lord is one with him in spirit." The Holy Spirit is literally married to our spirit. I learned to listen to that inner voice and do what it said.

As time progressed, I began to hear the Holy Spirit speaking to me about things that were going on in my life, giving me specific directives on what He wanted me to do or where He wanted me to go. While that might sound a little odd at first, you should consider that the Bible is simply full of stories of men who were directed and given instructions by the Holy Spirit. In the book of Acts, as church leaders were fasting and praying about the future, the Holy Spirit told them to appoint Paul and Barnabas as missionaries and send them out to plant churches. In another New Testament account, Jesus' disciple Peter was on a rooftop praying. He saw a vision and then heard the Holy Spirit say, "Simon, three men are looking for you. So get up and go downstairs. Do not hesitate to go with them, for I have sent them" (Acts 10:19b-20 NIV). In these stories from the Bible, each time the Holy Spirit spoke to someone and led them to do something, the results were always amazing.

As I look back over my life from that moment forward, my mind is flooded with key times that the Holy Spirit spoke very specifically to me and completely redirected my life, bringing me into new levels of fruitfulness. I remember the time when the Holy Spirit spoke to me as I was riding down a moonlit country road on my Harley, on my way home after a church softball game. He said to me, "I want you to quit your job and go to Christ for the Nations Institute in Dallas, Texas. I have a wife for you there." Then He told me to take a good friend of mine with me. He told me, "I have a special plan for his life as well." In response to His leading, I promptly quit my job, and my friend and I went to Bible College. I ended up marrying the assistant dean of women. My friend got a new call to the ministry. He changed all the plans he had made for his life and became a missionary. After a number of years on the mission field, he returned to the United States and became the lead pastor of a very large church and the head of a whole association of churches, covering several states.

A New Way to Live

Being led by the Holy Spirit is a really exciting, awesome way to live. God's plan for our life is not boring. So many people live on a much lower plane by not following His leading every day. I remember one incident that occurred when I was a construction worker, early in my marriage. I was laid off and low on money. My wife's parents called from out-of-state (they lived over one thousand miles away from us), and invited us to a very special family reunion. We had very little money. I added it all up - which didn't take long - and realized we had maybe enough for gas to get down to Louisiana from Michigan, but would have no money to get home. Being a newlywed, I certainly didn't want to put insecurity in my wife's parents' minds, and let them see how short I was on cash. On top of the gas money issue, I had an old car that was on its last legs. I prayed about what to do, and I clearly remember the Holy Spirit saying, "Go, and you will come home with more money than you left with."

Since I was a young Christian, I was very excited to have this kind of direction, and I immediately decided to travel down to the reunion with my wife. We barely made it there, and in spite of the leading I had felt from the Holy Spirit, I started to really wonder how we were going to get home. Around the middle of the week, my parents-in-law got a call from the pastor of their church saying, "I hear your son-in-law and daughter are in town." He went on to invite me to preach at their Wednesday night church service. Of course, I eagerly accepted. They took a small offering for me and it was almost exactly the same amount I had left home with. While that was encouraging, I remember thinking, as we began the drive home, "Holy Spirit, I thought I heard you say I would return home with *more* than I left with?" I wasn't being arrogant. I was just reflecting on it all, wondering about what I had heard.

Shortly thereafter, the tailpipe and muffler fell off our car as we hit the edge of Memphis. I thought, "Oh boy, now I'm really in trouble." With sparks flying, I pulled our old blue chariot onto an exit and into a nearby service center. I was told we needed a new piece of tail pipe and some connectors to hook the muffler back up. That would take almost all the rest of our money, leaving nothing more for gas. Not having much of a choice, I told them to fix it, and then went next-door with the last few pennies we had and sat at a Wendy's restaurant with my wife. We ate a burger while I contemplated our plight.

As I sat there, in a town I had never been to in my life, something very unexpected happened. A man in a black suit came walking across the parking lot. He opened the door of the restaurant and looked around; then, he stared at me and walked directly up to me. He simply said, "The Holy Spirit sent me here and said there was someone I was supposed to give some money to." He pulled out a wad of bills and pressed it into my hand. He then told me he was aware that we had car problems, and he had already been next-door to pay the bill. He told me his name was Brother Dick. He also was wearing a sort of clerical collar. He kind of looked like a priest or an angel, or whatever. All I know is, after shaking hands with me and wishing me God's best, he turned and just walked away. I was dumbfounded. I could hardly believe it. It was simply miraculous, like a Bible story. My wife and I triumphantly climbed into our blue chariot and headed for home with more money than we had left with. That lesson, along with many others over the years, taught me to rely on the voice and leading of the Holy Spirit. Of course, we all have common sense and we are to use our minds to make good decisions in our daily lives, but the Holy Spirit adds another dimension that leads us far beyond our normal capacity.

New Languages

I think another one of the big mental barriers people have to being filled with the Holy Spirit is confusion and misunderstanding concerning the new spiritual ability to pray in another language which often comes with the infilling of the Holy Spirit. In practically every instance where the Bible talks about believers being filled with the Holy Spirit, it says that they began to pray and worship in an unknown language. I will give you one of a number of examples. In the New Testament, apostle Peter was sharing with people who had never heard the gospel. Acts 10:44-46 (NIV) says, "While Peter was still speaking these words, the Holy Spirit came on all who heard the message. The circumcised believers who had come with Peter were astonished that the gift of the Holy Spirit had been poured out even on Gentiles. For they heard them speaking in tongues and praising God."

Despite the fact that it is clearly laid out in scripture as part of the spiritual ability we receive from the Holy Spirit, it still sometimes tends to scare or intimidate people and makes them feel like they're a little bit off-kilter if they embrace or practice something like that. Somebody might say, "Well, isn't that kind of crazy, praying in an unknown language, not knowing what you're saying?" I can say firsthand, "No, that's not crazy at all." In fact, it makes a lot of sense when you break it down. By the way, at the gym I watch people run on a treadmill for 45 minutes or even an hour and never move from the same place, just doing the same thing over and over again. What are they doing? They are building up their physical stamina and a healthy, strong body. They don't think that's crazy! But when it comes to spiritual exercise, people change up the rules because it doesn't seem normal.

From the spiritual aspect, I notice when I pray in another language that my spirit is being built up, just as though I am holding onto a battery charger. In fact, Jude 1:20 encourages believers in their prayer life to build themselves up in their most holy faith and praying in the Holy Spirit. This is the biblical definition for praying in an unknown tongue.

Actually, it's pure genius that God gave us a prayer language. Our mind can only grasp so much, and it tends to become a bottleneck, limiting our ability to be used by the Holy Spirit to pray about anything, anywhere, anytime. 1 Corinthians 14:14 (NLT) states, "For if I pray in tongues, my spirit is praying, but I don't understand what I am saying." This may sound like a senseless statement; however, if I had to think or know about every situation I pray about, it would tie up my mind. It would also greatly restrict other things I needed to think about and do at the moment. After I received this spiritual ability, I found I could pray all the time. It didn't matter where I was or what I was doing; now I could pray while my mind remained free to engage in the tasks at hand. I prayed while I was on hold on the phone, listening to elevator music, or biking, or out on the lake fishing. I had always wondered about the verse in the Bible that says we are to pray without ceasing. Whatever that meant, it surely meant doing a lot more praying than I had ever done before. But now a river of life had been unlocked in my inner being. Prayer just poured out of me, with virtually no effort at all, in a very natural way.

One other thing I noticed was that while I prayed on a more continual basis in the Spirit, my mind worked much better than before. I was constantly receiving illumination concerning God's direction for me, along with creative thoughts and inspiring ideas. I truly believe God illuminates our minds as we connect to Him in the spiritual realm through prayer in the Spirit. 1 Corinthians 14:15 (NIV) states, "So what shall I do? I will pray with my spirit and I will pray with my understanding." This shows us two ways to pray. There are great advantages to praying both ways. As I look back over my life, I can say that it is the infilling of the Holy Spirit that has enabled me to accomplish some amazing things that I had no chance of attaining on my own, not even in my wildest dreams.

If you have not yet been filled with the Holy Spirit, I would like to pray with you. I have a short, personal podcast that I have made for you and for anyone who wants to be filled with the Holy Spirit. I take a few minutes to explain it all, and then I personally pray for you to be filled with the Holy Spirit and help you receive your prayer language. Just go to rock-fordres.org/hsbaptism and I will spend some personal time praying with you. It will be one of the most important things you have ever done. The Holy Spirit will revolutionize your entire life, and empower you to become someone you never could be without Him.

Take Away:

God has called each one of us to be His witnesses and share the gospel of Jesus Christ. This daunting mission can seem impossible when we consider our own weak nature, fear, and insecurity. This is precisely why God offers us the gift of the Holy Spirit. Jesus said that we will receive power when the Holy Spirit comes upon us. The infilling or baptism of the Holy Spirit provides power and equips us with spiritual gifts that allow us to receive greater spiritual sensitivity and understanding.

We also gain new spiritual ability to pray in another language. In other words, you have the ability to pray in your known language as well us in the language of men and angels as stated in 1 Corinthians 13:1. Our new prayer language greatly increases our capacity to pray about anything and everything, including things we don't even know about. Praying in the spirit also builds up our inner man, bringing guidance and illumination to our minds. The baptism of the Holy Spirit allows us to live a life that is led by the Spirit, not just by our minds and intellect. The key to receiving the baptism of the Holy Spirit is to ask for it, and receive it by faith.

Discussion:

1. What fears, challenges, or insecurities do you face when attempting to share your faith with others?

2. The Holy Spirit provides you a new supernatural ability to share God's words and your personal testimony (even if you're not a people person). How does this challenge your willingness and ability to witness to others and follow God's plan for your life?

3. As you reflect on your own spiritual journey, who sits in the driver's seat the most - the Holy Spirit or you? Why can allowing the Holy Spirit to lead your life be challenging?

4. Have you received the infilling of the Holy Spirit? If so, how has life been different since you received the Holy Spirit? If not, what do you feel is holding you back from receiving the baptism of the Holy Spirit?

Activate Your Faith:

- Watch.. how to receive the infilling of the Holy Spirit by visiting www.rockfordres.org/hsbaptism

- Start praying for the unsaved and seek out opportunities to share your faith with them. (Consider making a prayer list that you can review daily).

- Memorize and ponder the following scripture verses:

  o *"But when he, the spirit of truth comes, he will guide you into all truth. He will not speak on his own, he will speak only when he hears, and he will tell you what is yet to come"* (John 16:13 NIV).

  o *"If you then, though you are evil, know how to give good gifts to your children, how much more will your Father in heaven give the Holy Spirit to those who ask him!"* (Luke 2:13 NIV).

  o *"But you will receive power when the Holy Spirit comes upon you. And you will be my witnesses, telling people about me everywhere..."* (Acts 1:8a NLT).

- Watch the podcast http://rockfordres.org/watch/message/ageofthechurch

- Watch podcast. Being led by the Holy Spirit 8/10/14 at http://rockfordres.org/media/sermons/keystobeingledbytheholyspirit/

Chapter 4
Dealing with the Devil

Very soon after you have turned from living your own way and stepped into a new life, you will encounter an enemy who stands against everything that has happened to you. All my life I had heard about the devil and from time to time even told jokes about him. I knew that he was generally behind all of the evil in the world, but I had never embraced the fact that he is an invisible, *personal* enemy who is dedicated to harassing and destroying me and my relationship with God. As believers in and followers of Christ, we were once lost human beings, separated from God by our sin, but now we are forgiven. We are right with God, and we have been empowered by the Holy Spirit to live a new life. Colossians 1:13-14 (NIV) says, "For he [God] has rescued us from the dominion of darkness and brought us into the kingdom of the Son he loves, in whom we have redemption and forgiveness of sins." It's very important for us to know that we have been completely delivered from Satan's power and from the sentence of death and judgment that hangs over him and his entire fallen kingdom.

Another important thing for us to know is the fact that even though Satan was legally defeated at the cross and, therefore, has no legal hold on us, he continues to operate illegally, in guerrilla warfare. He is still trying to attack our minds with thoughts and temptations in an attempt to draw us back into our old lifestyle and old way of doing things. 1 Peter 5:8-9 (NIV) says, "Be alert and of a sober mind. Your enemy the devil prowls around like a roaring lion looking for someone to devour. Resist him, standing firm in the faith..." Your newfound faith in Christ is a shield that you can use to protect yourself from the accusing thoughts the enemy may try to inject into your mind. Ephesians 6:16 (NIV) states, "In addition to all this, take up the shield of faith, with which you can extinguish all the flaming arrows of the evil one." The devil will still try to inject thoughts (referred to here as "flaming arrows") into your mind to make you feel guilty about your past mistakes and even things you are still struggling to put behind you; however, you are forgiven. You are not guilty, and you must resist these thoughts by memorizing and meditating on what the Word of God says about you. It states that you are utterly free and forgiven because of what Jesus did for you. The Word of God is a spiritual weapon. Ephesians 6:17b calls it a "spiritual sword" that has power to cut off any accusing thought that comes our way.

A favorite Scripture that I quote all the time is Romans 8:1-2 (NIV) which says, "Therefore, there is now no condemnation for those who are in Christ Jesus, because through Christ Jesus the law of the Spirit who gives life has set you free from the law of sin and death." As a new Christian, I quoted this verse over and over and meditated on it. I learned to recognize temptations and negative thought patterns that pulled me in the wrong direction. I pushed guilty, condemning thoughts out of my mind. I memorized and quoted verses that stated who I am in Christ. I found myself more and more embracing the reality that I am God's child, not the devil's property. He is my Father, my Dad. His love is unconditional. He won't reject me or condemn me, even if I fall flat on my face and completely fail in some area. I love the amazing redemptive story in the New Testament where Peter, one of Jesus' disciples, denied Jesus three times, accompanied by cursing and swearing. It was a seemingly unforgivable sin, committed three times in a row, back-to-back. After the time of crisis was over, Peter wept in shame for what he had done. I'm sure that the devil was right there, condemning Peter for his weakness and failure, telling him that it was all over and that he was no longer a child of God. But Jesus completely forgave and restored Peter. He reaffirmed His great love for Peter and recommissioned him as one of His most important personal representatives.

No Sin Can Separate us from God

I remember talking to a soldier who related one of his horrific experiences in wartime. He had been put in an impossible situation of being ordered to execute some people who had been conducting guerrilla warfare and acts of terrorism that had been traced to a particular village. Some of the suspects were children. When he refused to follow orders, his commander pulled out his gun and directed the soldier to follow his orders or be shot on the spot. It was an agonizing, high-pressure moment: follow orders in a time of war and kill, or be killed yourself. As I spoke with the man, I realized he was in agony as he shared his guilt for not taking a bullet himself. Instead, he followed the order he was given, which deeply violated his conscience. As a result, he felt God was offended with him and that he could not have a relationship with God because of what he had been forced to do. I must say in all my years, I have never seen such pain and guilt on a man. There he stood, shaking and weeping.

The Holy Spirit showed me that an evil spirit of guilt and condemnation was oppressing him with the intent of ruining his life with tormenting lies that would eventually push him toward suicide.

The first thing I did with this man was to tell him that God would be eager and more than willing to forgive him. I reminded him that the list of the main characters in the Bible reveals what could easily be called a "rogues' gallery": a long list of men and women who committed atrocities. Moses, David, and apostle Paul were all murderers. Aaron, the high priest for Israel, made a golden calf which led Israel into idol worship. Samson, the strong man who was a judge for Israel, had a fatal attraction to a woman from a nation of idol worshipers. Rahab, King David's great, great grandmother, was a former prostitute. Joseph's brothers, who eventually became the heads of the twelve tribes of Israel, hated their brother Joseph. They threw him in a pit and sold him as a slave. Then they lied to their father and broke his heart, saying a wild animal had killed Joseph. However, everyone in this list eventually repented from their sins and received God's forgiveness. They went on to become great men and women who shaped our spiritual history. I was able to pray with the young man. As we prayed, God broke off the evil spirit of guilt that was constantly accusing and condemning him in his mind, and he received God's peace and forgiveness. Shortly thereafter, he was filled with the Holy Spirit and is now on the new path that God offers to all who will come to Him; He simply won't turn anyone away. John 6:37 (NIV) states, "All those the Father gives me will come to me, and whoever comes to me I will never drive away."

Live in Freedom, Not Guilt

As time went on, I learned to reject every thought of guilt and condemnation in my own life. I developed a real knowing that nothing can separate me from the love of God. Here is another quote from the Bible that has given me great comfort and security, especially after I have messed up in some area. "He does not treat us as our sins deserve, or repay us according to our iniquities. For as high as the heavens are above the earth, so great is his love for those who fear him; as far as the east is from the west, so far has he removed our transgressions from us." (Psalm 103:10-12 NIV) The devil and his lying spirits want to keep us under guilt and condemnation, even though we are God's children. He knows if he can do that, we will not have peace in our hearts, and we will be weak and powerless. One of the most important things we can ever know about being a child of God is that He has forgiven *all* of our sins. He loves us unconditionally. His grace towards us is immeasurable. We are no longer children of the devil, and even though God wants us to live godly lives that please Him, that is not the foundation of our relationship with God. He loved us first. He has totally wiped our slate clean, and we are His children. We are forgiven and free. It's not because of our good deeds or our success, but because of what Jesus did for us on the cross.

I have been a believer now for many years. I have grown spiritually and done many good works. God has used me in many wonderful ways, but I will tell you that one thing has never changed. I know now, more than ever, that I will not stand before God someday and tell Him all the good things I did. I won't say, "See how good I am." That definitely will not be good enough. I will be there, humbly dependent on what Jesus did for me on the cross. That will always be the basis of my relationship with God. I love the words to the hymn that say:

> My hope is built on nothing less, than Jesus' blood and righteousness.

> I dare not trust the sweetest frame [*the best light that could be put on my own actions*], but wholly lean on Jesus' name.

On Christ the solid rock I stand. All other ground is sinking sand.

(*My Hope is Built on Nothing Less* by Edward Mote)

Here is a powerful confession that I make all the time about my life and my relationship with God. It is based on what the Bible says about us. I urge you to memorize it and quote it every day until it becomes an indelible part of your thought pattern.

Confession

My body is a dwelling place for the Holy Spirit, redeemed, cleansed, and sanctified (set apart) by the Blood of Jesus. My body is yielded to God for His service and for His glory. The devil has no place in me, no power over me, no unsettled claims against me. All has been settled by the Blood of Jesus. I belong to God. I have eternal life and I am a member of God's eternal family, and nothing can separate me from the love of Jesus. Amen.

Take Away:

There is nothing more the devil despises than when a person makes any decision that strengthens their relationship with God. Choosing to follow Christ is no exception! The devil is dedicated to harassing and destroying your relationship with God by driving lies and distractions into your mind that create spiritual wedges between you and God. The devil, however, has no real power over your mind or spirit, because Jesus paid for all our sins on the cross. Because of this, we are no longer facing the penalty of God's judgment. The enemy has no hold over us, nothing to hang over us, and we are no longer subject to the same judgment he faces. We are no longer in darkness. We belong to a different kingdom, a different family. This means that we can deflect the attacks of the devil with our faith, just as it says in Ephesians 6:16 (NIV): "In addition to all this, take up the shield of faith, with which you can extinguish all of the flaming arrows of the evil one."

With the leading of the Holy Spirit, we continually learn to identify and reject every thought of guilt and condemnation created by the devil. We can celebrate the work of the cross, knowing that there is nothing that can separate us from the love of God, regardless of how hard the devil may try!

Discussion:

1. In the days, weeks, or months following your decision to follow Jesus, did you feel like your journey moving forward was going smoothly or was it a little bumpy or even terribly rocky? Describe your experience.

2. Romans 8:35-39 (NIV) says: *"Who shall separate us from the love of Christ? Shall trouble or hardship or persecution or famine or nakedness or danger or sword?*

As it is written: 'For your sake we face death all day long; we are considered as sheep to be slaughtered.' No, in all these things we are more than conquerors through him who loved us. For I am convinced that neither death nor life, neither angels nor demons, neither the present nor the future, nor any powers, neither height nor depth, nor anything else in all creation, will be able to separate us from the love of God that is in Christ Jesus our Lord." How does this passage of scripture offer us hope for today and hope for the days ahead of us?

3.   What thoughts or lies from the devil do you need to cast out of your mind and break free from?

Activate your Faith:

- Read Ephesians 6:10-18. Consider reading this verse at the beginning of each day and reflect on how you can "put on the armor of God."

- Memorize and ponder the following scripture verses:

    o   *"Be alert and of sober mind. Your enemy the devil prowls around like a roaring lion looking for someone to devour. Resist him, standing firm in the faith, because you know that the family of believers throughout the world is undergoing the same kind of sufferings"* (1 Peter 5:8-9 NIV).

    o   *"Submit yourselves therefore to God, resist the devil and he will flee from you"* (James 4:7 NIV).

    o   *"We demolish arguments and every pretension that sets itself up against the knowledge of God, and we take captive every thought to make it obedient to Christ"* (2 Corinthians 10:5 NIV).

o   *"He does not punish us for all our sins; he does not deal harshly with us, as we deserve. For his unfailing love toward those who fear him is as great as the height of the heavens above the earth. He has re-moved our sins as far from us as the east is from the west"* (Psalm 103:10-12 NLT).

Chapter 5
A New Family

"God decided in advance to adopt us into his own family by bringing us to himself through Jesus Christ. This is what he wanted to do and it gave him great pleasure" (Ephesians 1:5 NLT).

My son Jonathan and his wife Kelley got an opportunity to adopt a baby boy. His birth father was from Zimbabwe, and his birth mother was from the United States. The adoption process was very complicated, with lots of red tape and many up and down moments. And lots of waiting. After a long, emotional roller coaster ride and many moments of uncertainty, there came a day when the whole family went to court and stood before the judge. An official legal announcement of adoption was made, and little

Joe became an official member of our family. His uncertain future became certain. He stepped into a new family who will provide love, security, and a support structure that will shape him for time and eternity.

The exact same thing happens to everyone who turns from their old way of life and accepts God as their new Father. We become members of a whole new family. God's Word says, "...you received God's Spirit when he adopted you as his own children, now we call him 'Abba,[dad] Father'" (Romans 8:15b NLT). A new future that is full of opportunity opens up. Suddenly, everyone who has ever accepted Jesus as their Savior becomes your brother and your sister. It's a massive spiritual family that covers the globe, and just like that, you are now part of it. You have a role to play, a purpose to fulfill. You wonder, "How do I relate to this new family? Where is my spot on the field? What can I bring to this family? How do I figure that out?" Let me give you some specific keys regarding how to relate to your new family.

When I turned my life over to God, I found that a new desire to serve Him welled up inside me. I wanted to do something for God and be a part of what He was doing. The first thing I knew I was supposed to do was to get together with other believers and worship God. The Bible instructs us to pursue fellowship with other believers and to build each other up. It also warns us against being isolated. Hebrews 10:25 (NLT) says, "And let us not neglect our meeting together, as some people do, but encourage one another, especially now that the day of his return is drawing near." Ecclesiastes 4:9-12 (NLT) goes on with some more practical advice and reasoning concerning our need to have our lives intertwined with other believers. It states:

> "Two people are better off than one, for they can help each other succeed. If one person falls, the other can reach out and help. But someone who falls alone is

in real trouble. Likewise two people lying close together can keep each other warm. But how can one be warm alone? A person standing alone can be attacked and defeated, but two can stand back to back and conquer. Three is even better, for a triple braided cord is not easily broken."

Finding a good church that is full of life and that feels right to you is a very important step in your walk with God. Ask Him to lead you to the right place. When you find a church like that, check to make sure that its basic beliefs are founded on the Bible. If everything lines up in your spirit and feels right, join it. Become a member.

At the time that I returned home, my father had just recently started a new church in a public building that he rented on the weekends. He had formerly been the pastor of a well-known denominational church. As he worked to get his "startup" venture moving forward, he asked me to help him with the music and setup of the sound system, chairs arranged for services, and pretty much anything else that needed to be done. I remember cleaning restrooms, picking up cigarette butts, and sweeping the parking lot - along with vacuuming the carpet. The building had typically been used for wedding receptions and parties earlier in the weekend, and you can imagine the aftermath of such events.

As I write this now, I am the pastor of a large church that has an awesome staff, worship team, and hundreds of people serving. We are reaching out beyond our walls to help hurting people and impact our entire community. Looking back, I can say with certainty that the beginning of my journey to finding my place in God's family started with going to a local church and finding something to do, and then just pitching in and serving. Starting out like that and working in any capacity felt so good to me. I met new friends and developed new relationships. I felt fulfillment and a sense that I was engaged in an active role that would continue to grow as time went on.

Start Small (Perhaps), But Start

I think that the key to finding your purpose and the exact spot for you within God's family starts with joining a local church and serving. The journey to my current role of influence started all the way on the other end of the spectrum with cleaning restrooms and sweeping parking lots. I believe doing those things brought a sense of humility and helped develop the heart of a servant in me. I found that when I got moving and made commitments to serve, God very naturally moved me into the exact spot I needed to be in so I could learn what I would need to know or use at a later time. I remember getting a job at a furniture factory when I was younger. My job was packing furniture into boxes at the end of the assembly line - the junior position that everyone new began with. But as time went on, I worked my way down the assembly line, doing different jobs and learning different things. Finally, a year later, I ended up being the one who built the main frames for the furniture, completely at the other end of the line. I and others in my position set the pace for the entire operation.

I want to encourage everyone, including you, to step out of your comfort zone. Find an entry point for serving. Don't be a spectator. Get in the game, and God will begin to move you into the exact place you need to be. There are so many ways to engage in serving in the local church. Maybe you are an organizer, a musician, or a Sunday school teacher. If you are an outgoing, hospitable person you could be an usher or a greeter. Maybe you feel called to be part of the prayer team. Maybe you are a business person who is really good with money. Start giving of yourself on a regular basis, related to the capacity with which God has blessed you. I promise you one thing—if you start serving and giving in a local church, it will be the doorway to a fruitful life and future for you and your family. I would add that cultivating the discipline of attending worship services regularly and serving with your whole family will impact your family's future in an amazing way. It will bring a security and stability that can be found in no other way. My own family is living proof that this principle is true.

A Dynamic Institution

The church is, first and foremost, God's family. Secondly, it is a dynamic, life-giving institution with a mission to help everyone we know to find the true pathway to God and eternal life. One thing I really love about today's younger generation is the fact that they don't want to sit around and play church. They want something that is real and dynamic, and when they find it, they want to get out and change their world and make a difference. I know our church is reaching out in every area to touch our community, our nation, and the world. In His great commission, Jesus told the church to go out into all the world and preach the gospel. The gospel means "good news," and that good news is that God will forgive our sins and give us a whole new life and purpose. We send mission teams to other countries. We send work teams to areas of great need in our own nation. We go downtown in our city. We have an outreach center that partners with many different food and clothing stores for those who are in need. We are able to take food and household goods to mobile home parks and other areas of need, along with carpenters and cleanup crews, and prayer teams. We are currently building a foster care support system for families who have adopted children or who are doing foster care. We have a goal to see all the children in our district placed in good homes. We have teams going into public schools, doing assemblies and mentorship programs. We have prayer going up for our nation and what is going on in our political arena. I don't mean to be rambling on here or bragging, but I haven't even gotten started with all the different areas of life our church is touching! There are many other churches across this country and the world who are doing a lot more than we are, but we are doing our best. And, altogether, we make up the universal family of God.

An Ultimate Purpose

There is one final, supreme purpose that God has for the church that is important for us to know. Ephesians 3:10-11 (NIV) states, "His intent was that now, through the church, the manifold wisdom of God should be made known to the rulers and authorities in the heavenly realms, according to his eternal purpose that he accomplished in Jesus Christ our Lord."

These verses contain an amazing revelation as to God's ultimate purpose for the church. It reveals the fact that God intends to show the devil and his fallen angels that good triumphs over evil, right triumphs over wrong. Love is stronger than hate, and forgiveness is more powerful than revenge. God is going to prove that His plan, His way, and His love and grace are the highest things in the universe. Ultimately, He wants to prove this to the devil and his cohorts *through our lives*. We have to turn our backs on the world, and deny the pull of the old nature that used to control us. We have to choose God's way instead of our own way. When we do these things, we prove to the devil that people will love God for who He is and what He has done for them, no matter what they have to go through.

The blood of those who have been persecuted and killed for their faith throughout the centuries stands as a testimony that there is a group of people on earth who love God more than their own lives and their own welfare. Every time we make good, godly choices to do right instead of wrong, we disprove Satan's claims about the human race, and we systematically validate God's way as the best way. Satan believes that he can control our lives using the pull and power of sin and the sensual age we live in. He believes he can keep us under his control by tempting us to sin. He believes we will choose a life of sin, choosing to do our own thing over living a life dedicated to God. But there is one group of people - called "the church" - who have been called out of darkness.

Colossians 1:13-14 (NIV) says, "For he [God] has rescued us from the dominion of darkness and brought us into the kingdom of the Son he loves, in whom we have redemption." In Greek terminology, the church is called the *Ekklesia*, meaning "the called out ones." They (we) stand together from every race, tribe, and language throughout history. We are God's family and we all shine as bright lights in a dark world, showing others the pathway to knowing God and to eternal life. In John 13:35 (NLT) Jesus said, "Your love for one another will prove to the world that you are my disciples." The true church of Jesus provides visible proof that God's love and His ways are supreme, and the devil's claims are utterly false and inferior.

This idea is of the highest importance: if you are going to thrive in your walk with God and achieve your ultimate purpose in this life, it is extremely important to make sure that your life is intertwined with other believers and that you are part of a church that's alive and well. Together, we need to always remember that God's plan for us is to be directly involved. He has an exact place for us in His family, and together we are extending God's grace and His divine influence into every area of life. Jesus told us, "You are the light of the world—like a city on a hilltop that cannot be hidden. No one lights a lamp and then puts it under a basket. Instead, a lamp is placed on a stand, where it gives light to everyone in the house." (Matthew 5:14-15 NLT)

Take Away:

We are members of God's family! When we join a local church family, we are combining our talents and assets with those already in place and together, and we strengthen the expression of that particular church. Over time, as we grow in grace, our lives are knit together with other believers. We find new friends, along with fellowship and encouragement. We learn how to apply principles from God's Word through the messages we hear. And finally, we impact the world around us by representing the life, love, and power of Jesus Christ. This is our collective purpose in this life as sons and daughters of God.

Discussion:

1. The Bible teaches that God is a father to the fatherless, a defender of the widows, and the One who provides a family for those who are lonely. His love is perfect - His love for us never fails! Is it hard to believe these promises from God in light of seeing your own earthly father fail you?

2. Do you feel that you are connected to God's family? In other words, have you begun to get to know your new family through church activities or Bible studies? How has (or how might) building those relationships help you in your growth as a new believer?

3. When God created you, He also gifted you to accomplish great work that He planned for you long ago. Think about and then share how God has uniquely gifted you to serve His people. (Tip: find a way to use your gifts to serve God's children in your local church)

Activate Your Faith:

- Does your church offer small groups or Bible studies? Join one, and begin to build relationships within your church family.

- Sign up to volunteer your gifts and time at your church. Remember, where you start will not necessarily be where you end. The important thing is that you start somewhere.

- Memorize and ponder the following scripture verses:

  o *"And let us not neglect our meeting together, as some people do, but encourage one another, especially now that the day of his return is drawing near"* (Hebrews 10:25 NLT).

  o *"In the same way, let your light shine before others, that they may see your good deeds and glorify your Father in heaven"* (Matthew 5:16 NIV).

  o *"God has given each of you a gift from his great variety of spiritual gifts. Use them well to serve one another"* (1 Peter 4:10 NLT).

Chapter 6
Shipwreck

"Cling to your faith in Christ, and keep your conscience clear. For some people have deliberately violated their consciences, as a result, their faith has been shipwrecked" (1 Timothy 1:19 NLT).

I'm outta here."

That was the abrupt response of the young man who had come forward to ask me to pray for him. To backtrack a bit, he had just asked me to pray for him to be able to get his children back. To get some background, I asked what the situation was. He told me his ex-wife had gotten total custody of his children and now she was going to move out of state. He would not be able to see them on a regular basis any longer. He again asked me to pray that he would get them back. Instead, I asked him another brief question about the situation. His reply revealed that it was a complex situation that did not favor him, mostly because of his mistakes. I started to tell him that his request for prayer wasn't quite that simple. I told him I could not just pray some simple prayer that would cancel all the mistakes and dysfunctional things that had happened. I told him I would be happy to meet with him and give some good counsel on things he could do to get back into a healthy place with his broken family. The young man said, "Look, I came up here with a prayer request. I'm not interested in a whole bunch of advice." And just like that, he turned and walked out. I turned to his current girlfriend who still stood there, somewhat embarrassed by the whole scene. I said, "So, you stayed?" She said, "Yes." I said, "Do you want me to give *you* some advice?" She again said, "Yes." I said, "If I were you, I would run for my life and never look back." To the best of my knowledge, she followed my advice.

This story is both sad and somewhat humorous. In any case, it serves as a great example of what happens to so many people in their walk with God, especially in the early stages. They turn their lives over to Christ and start following Him, but sooner or later something happens. A snag comes, due to a misconception about who God is or how they expect Him to work in their life. Or, it could come from another believer who offends them in some way. Ultimately, when someone is offended it becomes something that separates them from God or from fellowship with other believers. This is a very dangerous thing because if something is not done it can destroy their faith and their relationship with God completely.

Jesus told a parable in the New Testament book of Matthew about a farmer who went out to sow seed. This allegorical story describes four types of ground, which represent the various heart conditions of people who hear God's Word. The farmer who sows the seed represents the person who shares God's Word. The seed that is scattered on the ground represents the Word of God, and the truth about His desire to offer us salvation and a new way to live. The first type of ground is the highway or the wayside. The second type of soil is called the "stony ground." The third type of soil is the thorny ground, full of weeds. The fourth type of ground is called "good ground," with no stones and no weeds. After telling the story, Jesus offered a full explanation of its meaning in Matthew 13:18-23 (NLT):

> "Now listen to the explanation of the parable about the farmer planting seeds: The seed that fell on the footpath represents those who hear the message about the Kingdom and don't understand it. Then the evil one comes and snatches away the seed that was planted in their hearts. The seed on the rocky soil represents those who hear the message and immediately receive it with joy. But since they don't have deep roots, they don't last long. They fall away as soon as they have problems or are persecuted for believing God's word. The seed that fell among the thorns represents those who hear God's word, but all too quickly the message is crowded out by the worries of this life and the lure of wealth, so no fruit is produced. The seed that fell on good soil represents those who truly hear and understand God's word and produce a harvest of thirty, sixty, or even a hundred times as much as had been planted!"

I believe this story is very important for us to understand. Obviously, the first kind of ground represents those who hear the Word of God, but it never takes root. The devil lies to the person and tells them the things of God are not for them. Their hearts are not affected at all and they remain unchanged—completely separated from God. The rocky ground is very concerning. It represents those who do become believers and start to follow God, but then they run into trouble. Something happens that they don't expect. Someone says or does something to hurt their feelings. In other situations, some begin to claim the promises of God's Word and pray for Him to help them or meet their needs. When things don't happen the way they expect, they become disillusioned with God and develop an offense with Him. They don't understand their new Father and how He operates.

Blind Faith

As an example of this type of misunderstanding, when I first discovered the truth about healing in the Bible, I began to hear ministers teach on the fact that God still heals people today. I saw promises in the Word concerning healing. Isaiah 53:5 (KJV) states, "But he [Jesus] was wounded for our transgressions, he was bruised for our iniquities: the chastisement of our peace was upon him; and with his stripes [whiplash wounds] we are healed." In the great commission, Jesus said that the ability to pray effectively for healing was one of the signs that someone was a believer. Mark 16:18b (NIV) says, "…they will lay their hands on sick people, and they will get well." I was a very young believer when I first discovered some of these things. I immediately began to believe God for healing in my life and in the lives of others. I remember thinking to myself, "Why am I wearing glasses, when God can heal my eyes?" I promptly claimed healing for my eyes. I believed God for my healing, based on the Bible verses about healing. I went down to the Grand River, not too far from my house, and ceremoniously threw my glasses off a bridge. For the next couple of weeks, I stumbled around half blind, expecting any moment that a miracle would hit me. That did not happen. I must tell you, I was somewhat offended by that fact. As a result of this experience, I remember feeling very insecure for a period of time about stepping out in faith in other areas of my life. I remember feeling that God had let me down when I had come to Him in sincerity, with my best effort. Fortunately, I had a godly mother who gave me some very wise advice. She said, "Son, if you are believing God for something and it doesn't happen that way, or it doesn't happen at all, just remember one thing—there is nothing wrong with God. There is nothing wrong with His Word. He is your divine Father and His Word is eternal and true."

A Loving Father

Many times we develop a preconceived idea on how we expect God to work on our behalf. When something goes wrong and it doesn't work out the way we wanted, we are tempted to believe that His Word is not true or that He doesn't care as much about us as we thought. But that's a lie the devil wants you to believe. God promises many things to us in His Word, but there is a divine timing in the way that He gives us what we need. Much of the time, it's not in the way we would expect or in the timeframe we would expect. In the same sort of way, look at earthly parents and their children. What if the children just started asking their dad or mom for any old thing they wanted? They have many requests and desires. They want new toys, snacks, to stay up late, skip going to school, more money in their allowance, new clothes, a new bicycle, or new iPhones. The list goes on and on. Some things could be deemed necessary, others not so much. Very obviously, those of us who are parents understand that our children have wants, needs, and desires in multiple areas. We want to give them all that is necessary for them to have a great life and future; however, we understand the timing and the amount of provision that we provide is critical to their health and development, not to speak of discipline and correction. If this is true of earthly parents, can you imagine how much more important it is for God to do the same for His children? He has given us His Word concerning His love and care for us, along with His promises. He hears every request in our prayers and He will answer in His own way, in His own time.

There are times when we can pray with authority and certainty because we know exactly what God's will is. But many times we must also preface what we are asking and believing for with, "God, Your will be done." When Jesus was teaching His disciples how to pray, He gave them a model prayer that we call "The Lord's Prayer." One of the main phrases in that prayer is, "Your kingdom come, Your will be done, on earth as it is in heaven." Jesus Himself is the ultimate example of someone who asked God for help in a very critical time of His life. As a son, He had a right to ask His Father for help and deliverance. As He faced crucifixion, He was in the darkest, most painful hour of His life. He knew all the Bible promises about claiming divine protection and being delivered from evil. He prayed words to this effect: "Heavenly Father, please save me from this dark hour. If there's any other way than the cross for Your kingdom purposes to be accomplished, please let it happen that way instead. Nevertheless Your kingdom come, Your will be done" (Luke 22:42, author's paraphrase).

Every Prayer *is* Answered

This is the prayer we must pray, accompanied with that mindset in any situation or circumstance we find ourselves in. The bottom line is this: we will all have multiple chances to be offended by things that happen to us that we don't understand. When that happens, we need to make a decision to hang onto God no matter what. We must keep trusting Him fully and go for it with everything we have. I love the line in a popular song by Garth Brooks about a girl he was in love with. He prayed that God would give him that girl for his wife. But it didn't happen. He was heartbroken over the situation, but later on he met the exact girl of his dreams. As he looked back over his life, he realized that God had something much better in mind for him. The key line in the song says, "I thank God for unanswered prayers." Of course, I must state that God answers all prayers. It's just that sometimes, as in Garth's case, it's not always "yes." It could be *no*, or *not yet*, or *keep trusting Me and wait.*

A lady came into my office recently and wanted to see me. As we sat together, she poured out her heart and tears were running down her face. She said to me, "Pastor, I am going to leave my husband and just want you to understand why. I have been believing for him to commit his life to Christ for years, but nothing has happened. He gives me no support spiritually. There's just nothing. We have no fellowship. From time to time he comes to church with me and the kids, but he just sits there and doesn't respond. This has created a real spiritual void in our family and I just can't take it anymore. I have prayed and prayed and prayed and nothing has happened."

As I listened to her, I could see that she was at the end of her rope. She was frustrated and totally discouraged, and I really felt for her. I could tell she was somewhat disappointed with the fact that God had not touched her husband. She had spent much time in prayer and patience, waiting for him to come around, but nothing had happened. Deep down, I knew she was looking for some level of support from me in moving ahead with her decision. I asked her if her husband had been faithful to her and if he had been a good father and a provider for their family. Her answer was "yes." I told her that as much as I wanted to give her some encouraging word or support to move ahead with her decision, I could not. I told her she needed to stay with her husband and continue to hold on to God and trust Him for their future.

I went over what the Bible says about being married to someone who is not a believer. I showed her where 1 Corinthians 7:14 (ESV) says, "For the unbelieving husband is made holy because of his wife, and the unbelieving wife is made holy because of her husband. Otherwise your children would be unclean, but as it is they are holy." I went on to tell her that her relationship with God was providing a holy covering of God's grace for their entire family, regardless of her husband's condition, and that it was imperative that she stay in that place and not step out of it. Second, I told her what the Bible says concerning the challenge facing someone married to an unbeliever, and what to do about it. 1 Corinthians 7:12-13 & 16 (ESV) says, "To the rest I say this, (I, not the Lord) if any brother has a wife who is an unbeliever and, she consents to live with him, he should not divorce her. And if a woman has a husband who is not a believer and he is willing to live with her, she must not divorce him. For how do you know, wife, whether you will save your husband? Or how do you know, husband, whether you will save your wife?"

After explaining these things to her, I prayed with her that God would give her the grace to fully walk out the challenges that lay before her and not give up on her husband. I could tell she was somewhat disappointed with our meeting. She left my office sad, but knowing she needed to continue trusting God and soldier on. Two or three weeks later, at the end of one of our Sunday services, I gave a call for people to commit their lives to Christ. Her husband raised his hand and prayed to receive Christ as his Savior. He later told me how he had sat from week to week in our services and even enjoyed them to some degree. There was very good music and good, energetic speaking, but in it all, he felt no reason to enter into any type of spiritual commitment. He said that while he was listening to one particular message, though, something happened inside of him. Suddenly he understood what was happening at a whole new level and he said, "All my lights just went on." As I listened to him talk about being born again, I couldn't help but look into his wife's eyes, looking back at me over his shoulder while he was talking; one look said it all. She had come so close to missing it. Her marriage would have ended with everyone hurt on all sides. But, worst of all, her husband might have been lost forever. She made the right decision to obey God's Word about her marriage and family and avoided a potential shipwreck.

When things aren't working out at the moment, do not ever let yourself become offended with God by thinking that He doesn't care or He isn't listening to your prayers. Instead, I challenge you to do what I have learned to do. I switch to what I call my "big picture Bible verse," Romans 8:28 (NKJV), which states, "And We know that all things work together for good to those who love God, and to those who are called according to His purpose." This is a big picture promise from God for our lives and I must say, my own life proves it. I look back over every situation that I prayed about that didn't work out, and I realize that somehow God miraculously used it all to bring me to where I am today. All we need to do is keep moving forward and hang onto God and trust that in some way, He is working it all out. My father had a motto that I have adopted as my own. He said, "I will not be sidelined; I will not be benched; I will not be taken out of the game. If the coach makes me sit on the bench, I will polish bats and be the water boy. I will not let my life be rendered ineffective for God's kingdom and His service by anything or anyone." I think that is a fantastic model for every believer.

Rely on God

I want to challenge you to not let anything stop you. Go the distance. Find out what God's Word says about every area of your life and determine to follow the instructions it gives. There is no higher way to live. It is the pathway to true life that embraces eternity and goes on and on and on. And, lastly, I think it's good to remember one more thing. I think even the decision to hang onto God must be attributed to the grace of God working in our lives. I believe it is grace that gives us the strength to make the decision to hang on to God. In the end, it is the only thing we can give credit to for going the distance with God and His amazing grace.

Take Away

When God's Word is taken out of context, twisted to match our own motives or simply misunderstood, a misconception of who God is and how He operates in our lives can occur. These misconceptions can lead to an offense with God or an offense with other people, creating a separation in our relationship with God and others. This is why it is so important to find out what God's Word tells us and teaches us over every area of our life. Furthermore, we must commit to following the teachings and instructions God's Word gives us. When we fully rely on and trust in God's Word, God will give us the grace and strength to hang on through any circumstance. We can then stand firm against the enemy's attempts to use the tool of offense to separate us from God.

Discussion:

1. When God answers your prayers, have you found yourself disappointed with any of the answers that you received from God? Why or why not?

2. How well do you fully trust in God and in His Holy Word? What experiences have led you to trust or not to trust in God?

3. Forgiveness is the key to overcoming offense. When we choose to hold an offense, we are choosing unforgiveness. How has unforgiveness created a separation between you and God, or with others, either currently or in your past?

4. God's Word is our answer book. What questions do you need answered that will help you better understand who

God is and the relationship God desires to have with you?

5.

Activate Your Faith

- Write out all of the questions, doubts, or confusing scriptures that you would like to better understand. Find someone you can talk to at your church to help guide you through answering these questions.

- Memorize and ponder the following scripture verses:
  - *"Your word is a lamp for my feet, a light on my path"* (Psalm 119:105 NIV).

  - *"Bear with each other and forgive one another if any of you has a grievance against someone. Forgive as the Lord forgave you"* (Colossians 3:13 NIV).

  - *"Get rid of all bitterness, rage and anger, brawling and slander, along with every form of malice. Be kind and compassionate to one another, forgiving each other, just as in Christ God forgave you"* (Ephesians 4:31-32 NIV).

- Watch podcast –"Are You Offended?"
  http://rockfordres.org/watch/message/areyouoffended1

Chapter 7
Killing Private Enemy
Number One

"You were taught, with regard to your former way of life, to put off your old self, which is being corrupted by its deceitful desires; to be made new in the attitude of your minds; and to put on the new self, created to be like God in true righteousness and holiness" (Ephesians 4:22-24 NIV).

There is at least one other enemy to your new life that needs to be addressed. It is the old sinful, selfish nature that used to run your life. We inherited the old nature from Adam. After he and his wife, Eve, sinned by eating the fruit that God told them not to eat, all of their children and descendants were born with a rebellious nature that wanted to go its own way. One term to describe this nature would be "self-centered." The old nature is not yielded to anyone. The lyrics to an old hit pop song by the Animals called "It's my Life" expresses this inner nature very well. The song speaks about thinking or doing whatever you want to do, answerable to no one. Another song, penned by Ricky Nelson, called "Garden Party," talks about putting yourself ahead of everyone else when it comes to pleasure or fulfill-ment of any type. Music is a major voice in culture. It reveals the heart and soul of what's going on in each generation. From the 60's, 70's, and the 80's, and on up to this present time, music has been more and more open and blatant in revealing what's going on inside the human heart and mind. George Thorogood's "Bad to the Bone," along with AC/DC's "Hell's Bells" and "Back in Black," literally celebrate rebellion and self-seeking and laugh at the consequences. Pop and country music songs celebrate everything from binge drinking and girl crushes, to one night stands. Much of rap music promotes violence, rebellion and sexual prom-iscuity. Yes, there are some really good songs in each arena I have described as well, but for the most part they are being drowned out and minimized by the blatant, rebellious self-seeking nature of this age.

How Low Can You Go?

Following that old nature and its promptings will put a person on the highway to hell. Our old nature is self-cen-tered and rebellious, and if it is not controlled, it will always lead us downward into sinful patterns that are the opposite of anything God wants us to do. Our old nature wants to sleep in; it wants to overeat, worry, lie, lust, and steal. It wants to swear in anger at a driver who cuts us off. It wants to have outbursts of anger for no particular reason. It's jeal-ous. It's vengeful. It wants to gamble, gossip, cast off restraint, and overindulge. The list of vices and sinful compulsions goes on and on. A lot of these things can bring temporary pleasure and gratification, and it may feel good to call our own shots as to how we want to live, but in the end, we are still unfulfilled and empty. On top of that, we end up becoming enslaved to the very things we indulged in. From that point on, it's a long, dark, downward death spiral.

When we come to Christ, we receive a new nature and an inner desire to serve God and not follow the impulses of the old nature. 1 John 5:4 (NIV) says, "For everyone born of God overcomes the world. This is the victory that has overcome the world, even our faith." John also says, "…because greater is he that is in you, than he that is in the world" (1 John 4:4b KJV). That new nature is infinitely more powerful than the old selfish nature that used to run our lives. As we yield to that nature and follow God's plan, the old nature is dethroned and its penalty of eternal death - along with its power to rule over us in this life - is canceled.

Not Dead Yet

That said, I think it's very important to understand that although the old nature has been dethroned and sidelined, it's still there. It has a voice that still urges you to do your own thing and go your own way.

I recently heard a rather humorous story about a missionary who was riding his bicycle down the street to an appointment in the city. He encountered a boy pushing a lawnmower down the road with a sign on it that said, "For Sale." The missionary stopped and questioned the boy and asked, "Why are you selling your lawnmower?" The boy replied, "I am trying to come up with the money to buy a bicycle." The missionary thought for a moment and then he said to the boy, "Would you take my bicycle in trade for that lawnmower?" The boy said, "I don't know - let me try it out." So the boy took a little ride on the bike, back-and-forth down the road, and said, "Ok, you have yourself a deal." They exchanged items, and the missionary took the lawnmower and reached down and pulled the rope to start it. After several tries, the lawnmower did not start and the missionary said, "Hey, this lawn mower doesn't start." The boy said, "Oh yes, I forgot to tell you. To get it to start, you have to cuss at it." The missionary said, "Well, I don't cuss. In fact, it's been so long since I cussed that I don't even remember how to cuss." The boy replied, "Keep pulling that rope, and it will all come back to you."

One of the reasons the story is funny is because we know it's true. As Christians, we have a new nature, a new living hope, and a new future. But the old nature that the Bible calls "the flesh" is still there in the background, wanting to rear its ugly head and pull us back into the darkness. Galatians 5:17 (NIV) states, "For the flesh desires what is contrary to the Spirit, and the Spirit what is contrary to the flesh. They are in conflict with each other, so that you are not to do whatever you want." On top of that, the devil exploits the old nature and tries to get us to go back to listening to its voice. Sometimes this can be maddening.

Let me give you another common example of the inner conflict we all face. Take the situation of a Christian man walking down the street, where he encounters an attractive lady. She's a bit flirtatious and somewhat inappropriately dressed. She says "Hi" as they pass and gives him a little wink. Almost immediately, two different voices began to talk to him at once. One voice says, "This is a real opportunity for you - go for it." The other voice (which is the Holy Spirit speaking to his conscience) says, "This girl could be trouble, so mind your own business. Be polite and respectful and move on."

As another illustration, there might be a time when you get into a difficult situation and one voice says to you, "Tell a little lie and you can fix this thing." The other voice says, "Be honest." Or, one voice says, "Worry, worry, worry." The other voice says, "Trust God and don't worry about any-thing." And on and on it goes. Your new nature, powered by the Holy Spirit, is now on the throne of your life, but the old nature is still talking to you. The devil tries to exploit our old nature as he desperately tries to get us to go back to our old rebellious lifestyle.

Monkey on My Back

My son Daniel told me about an interesting method for hunting wild boars invented by the natives of Mozambique. They would train monkeys to work for them. As the story goes, they would go find a herd of wild pigs and they would release all the monkeys. The monkeys, who are a lot quicker than people, would run after a wild boar and jump on its back, distracting it and slowing it down considerably. Even-tually, another monkey would catch up and jump on the same animal for a ride, until multiple monkeys slowed the quarry down enough for the hunters to catch it. I actually watched a YouTube video of the whole hunting process. I found it to be both humorous (because of the methodology), and also somewhat sad as the animal struggled for its life. One moment the wild boar was wandering out on the prairie, totally free and enjoying its life. The next moment, it was frantically trying to escape capture and death. Meanwhile, on the other hand, the monkeys were having a great time enjoying a fun, free ride on the frantic animal's back.

This example reminded me of how Satan and his de-mons prowl around, looking for some way to exploit some weakness in our old nature and bring us back into captivity. 1 Peter 5:8 (NIV) says, "Be alert and of sober mind. Your enemy the devil prowls around like a roaring lion looking for someone to devour." Satan deploys one of his demonic monkeys to tempt us and lie to our minds. He desperately tries to slow us down by getting us to engage in a sinful thought pattern. If we don't identify his tactics, that harmful thought pattern will lead to sinful actions. As a result, we find that we end up with a monkey on our back, slowing us down and hindering our walk with God to the point that it encroaches on the freedom God's grace has provided. The end result is a life-and-death struggle to get back on the path of grace and forgiveness. The farther we go down the road of sin, the tighter the monkey digs in with his grip. Your unseen enemy whispers in your ear and says, "Look! You haven't changed. You're no different than you ever were. You're not a believer. You're not forgiven. It's all a fantasy. This is how you really are." There is an old line I've heard many times that says, "Sin will take you farther than you wanted to go, it will keep you longer than you wanted to stay, and cost you more than you intended to pay." There is a lot of truth in this statement.

Assassinate the Old Nature

I would like to give you the key to getting that monkey off your back and silencing the voice and influence of the old nature and any way the devil could exploit it. First and foremost, God's Word tells us what to do when we get in this situation—submit yourselves to God. Resist the devil and he will flee from you. (see James 4:7) Ultimately, there must come a point where we firmly decide to put sinful patterns behind us. This requires asking God to forgive us for following the impulses of the old nature. Second, we must resubmit that area of our life to God and say, "God, I'm going to follow Your standards in that area of my life and obey You." The next thing the Word says to do is "resist the devil and he will flee from you." The simplest way for me to tell you how to do this is to speak to the monkey on your back and say, "I resist your temptations and your lies. God has forgiven me. You are off my back and out of my life. Be gone, in Jesus' name." When you do that, you will feel the demonic pressure let up and weaken. However, this is not the end.

We must not stop there, but continue to push hard in whatever area we are being oppressed, until every ounce of that influence is gone. Every believer has power over the forces of darkness because the blood of Christ canceled Satan's claims on the cross. "He has delivered us from the power of darkness and conveyed us into the kingdom of the Son of His love, in whom we have redemption through His blood, the forgiveness of sins." (Colossians 1:13-14 NKJV). We are children of the light and when we speak the Word of God in faith, the enemy must let go and run.

Build Up Your New Nature

At times, we may feel overwhelmed in our struggle with patterns of sin that originate from our old nature. We go up and down, in and out, in our striving to be Godly. I was reading Mark Batterson's fantastic book simply titled, "If." He made a point in a subheading about building the new nature and resisting the old nature's influence that was so simple and straightforward that I must mention it. He said, "Strengthen your NO muscle." Everyone who is a child of God must learn to say "no" to temptation and the wayward impulses of the old nature. Romans 8:13 (NIV) states, "For if you live according to the flesh, you will die, but if by the Spirit you put to death the misdeeds of the body, you will live."

Ultimately, that means we have to get good at saying "no," and there is nothing that strengthens that ability like fasting from food. Saying "no" in this area starves and weakens the fleshly (bodily) drive and strengthens our spirit. Fasting is like throwing gas on the fire of our spiritual growth. I believe this is especially true in areas of weakness that we have. From time to time throughout my life I have fasted, sometimes a day, a week, or even for a longer period of time to get a handle on things that were getting the upper hand in my life. Each time I did this, I have experienced breakthroughs in my spiritual life. We must continually discipline ourselves to say "no." When we do this, we will win the inner conflict that goes on between flesh and spirit. We will experience true victory and start to enjoy our walk with God, instead of living in a tug of war, perpetually on the edge of victory and defeat.

A Mind Makeover

In the New Testament, apostle Paul gives us the ultimate challenge and the main key to our spiritual growth: a total transformation of the mind. Romans 12:1-2 (NIV) states:

> Therefore, I urge you, brothers and sisters, in view of God's mercy, to offer your bodies as a living sacrifice, holy and pleasing to God—this is your true and proper worship. Do not conform to the pattern of this world, but be transformed by the renewing of your mind. Then you will be able to test and approve what God's will is—his good, pleasing and perfect will.

You will notice that the central message in these verses is the fact that we need to be transformed. But how? *By the renewing of our minds*. Our minds need a total makeover. Over the period of many years, we develop thought patterns that we are very familiar with and which are connected to our old sinful nature and our old way of doing things. We need to retrain our minds as to what the truth of the Word of God says, and make a decision that His Word is what we are going to follow. His Word is what we are going to obey.

Take Every Thought Captive

Our thoughts are the origins of all our actions. When we activate our thoughts, they become our actions. When we repeat those actions, they become a habit, and eventually that habit becomes a lifestyle. The Bible tells us not to let one single thought float through our mind unaddressed. 2 Corinthians 10:5 (NIV) says, "We demolish arguments and every pretension that sets itself up against the knowledge of God, and we take captive every thought to make it obedient to Christ."

I stated earlier that the Word of God is a spiritual weapon. When we speak it, it has amazing spiritual power to cut off demonic-inspired thoughts and the tendencies of the old nature. Our faith is another spiritual tool. The Bible calls it "a shield" against demonic attacks in our thought life. Ephesians 6:16-17 (NIV) says, "In addition to all this, take up the shield of faith, with which you can extinguish all the flaming arrows of the evil one. Take the helmet of salvation and the sword of the Spirit, which is the Word of God."

Throughout this book, I have given you suggested scripture verses to memorize. If you will memorize every scripture at the end of each chapter, by the time you get to the end of this book, you will find that you have an arsenal of weaponry that will protect your mind and keep you on course with God's plan for your life.

When a thought from the old nature comes, you will recognize it and cut it off with the sword of God's Word. You will speak His divine standard. I encourage you to say the words out loud if you have to. I first identify the incoming thought as wrong. I arrest it and say, "The old nature that used to control me is dead. That's not me anymore. I'm a new person, and my life is dedicated to God. I am a member of the family of God. And I am following God's will for my life." When we do this consistently, it will cut off the power of old thought patterns and eventually all the feelings that go with it. More than once I have done these kind of things out loud, even driving down the road in my car. Occasionally, I have gotten some funny looks from other motorists, but I don't care. I'm in a war and by God's grace I am winning.

A negative thought process of anger or some covetous, lustful, or vindictive thought may knock at the door of your mind. It may be a demonic suggestion that the enemy wants you to buy into, or it may just be some fearful, worrisome old thought pattern that needs to be more thoroughly dealt with. Either way, I don't tolerate it. I address it and say no to that thought. That is not who I am, that thought is not what I'm about. I reject that thought. I am a new creation, holy, set apart. I'm not covetous, vengeful, lustful or vindictive, etc. Then I like to pause and worship God and thank Him for His grace and the power over the sinful nature and maybe even crank up a worship song to boost my spirit even more. It may seem strange that you are taking such extreme measures just to stop a certain thought process. But, if you do it a number of times, you will notice a marked difference in your thinking and your actions. You will clearly be able to distinguish between the old nature that used to control you and the new nature that is in you. You will grow stronger every day, and you will become confident and secure in your new life.

As we meditate on scripture and use it effectively against the old nature, it actually does become a "helmet of salvation." Our mind is covered and protected by renewed thought patterns that have been shaped through obedience to God's Word. We develop new instincts that are Godly. The end result is this—you will be killing private enemy number one and your old nature's voice will have a weak, hollow ring, like a doorbell ring that no one is answering.

I would like to share some of my favorite verses to memorize. They give us a mandate. They also describe our new life and purpose and the dethroned state of the old nature. I challenge you to memorize Colossians 3:1-3, then read the rest of the passage through verse 10. Start each day with this passage, for a month straight. Quote the first three verses out loud by memory, and then read the rest of the passage. After 30 days, it will be ingrained in your mind. It will change your life. It will change your focus. It will affect your actions and become another nail in the coffin of "private enemy number one."

"Since, then, you have been raised with Christ, set your hearts on things above, where Christ is, seated at the right hand of God. Set your minds on things above, not on earthly things. For you died, and your life is now hidden with Christ in God. When Christ, who is your life, appears, then you also will appear with him in glory. Put to death, therefore, whatever belongs to your earthly nature: sexual immorality, impurity, lust, evil desires and greed, which is idolatry. Because of these, the wrath of God is coming. You used to walk in these ways, in the life you once lived. But now you must also rid yourselves of all such things as these: anger, rage, malice, slander, and filthy language from your lips. Do not lie to each other, since you have taken off your old self with its practices and have put on the new self, which is being renewed in knowledge in the image of its Creator" (Colossians 3:1-10 NIV)

Take Away

Our old self-centered nature needs to be put to death. As we continually renew our minds, our lives will no longer be led by our sinful and rebellious "old nature," but rather, our lives will be submitted to our new nature and the inner desire to serve God. We must choose to yield to our new nature and silence the voice and influence of our old nature by taking every thought captive that the enemy places in our mind, and extinguish its power and influence with the Word of God. Through discipline and practice, when a thought from the old nature comes, you will recognize it, reject it, and take it captive with your secret weapon, the sword of God's Word.

Discussion

1. Describe your old nature. For example, was it rebellious? Angry? Lustful? Worrisome? Dishonest? Etc.

2. What does the conflict between your new nature and old nature look like today? If you had to say who's winning the battle, what would you say?

3. Do you feel like you are equipped with the right scripture to defeat your sinful nature? Why or why not?

4. What types of thoughts must you take captive and defeat with the Word of God?

Activate Your Faith

- What specific thoughts from the enemy must you take captive? Write them down. Then find a scripture (God's truth about the lie from the enemy), that you can use to defeat these destructive thoughts. Next to where you have written out the lie from the enemy, write the truth from God that contradicts it. Meditate on God's truth daily, until you have completely defeated the power and influence that these lies had in your life.

- Memorize and ponder the following scripture verses:

    o *"You were taught, with regard to your former way of life, to put off your old self, which is being corrupted by its deceitful desires; to be made new in the attitude of your minds; and to put on the new self, created to be like God in true righteousness and holiness" (Ephesians 4:22-24 NIV).*

    o *"Since, then, you have been raised with Christ, set your hearts on things above, where Christ is, seated at the right hand of God. Set your minds on things above, not on earthly things. For you died, and your life is now hidden with Christ in God" (Colossians 3:1-3 NIV).*

    o *"Therefore, I urge you, brothers and sisters, in view of God's mercy, to offer your bodies as a living sacrifice, holy and pleasing to God—this is your true and proper worship. Do not conform to the pattern of this world, but be transformed by the renewing of your mind. Then you will be able to test and approve what God's will is—his good, pleasing and perfect will" (Romans 12:1-2 NIV).*

- Watch podcast Killing the Shadow Man at http://rockfordres.org/media/sermons/killing-the-shadow-man/

Chapter 8
Hit You Where You Live

"...My child, don't make light of the Lord's discipline, and don't give up when he corrects you. For the Lord disciplines those he loves, and he punishes each one he accepts as his child" (Hebrews 12:5b-6 NLT).

O n your face, you [blankety-blank], or I'll blow your [blankety-blank] head off!" I stared down the gaping muzzle of the large caliber handgun shoved in my face and the crazy black eyes behind it, and I knew for sure the man behind the gun meant business. Suddenly, my friend and I were face down on the ice cold ground with our hands behind our backs. I tried to protest and ask why we were being apprehended, but again the screaming, crazy voice told me to "shut up or else." I knew I was in no position to argue, so we just laid on the frozen ground for over 20 minutes, with our hands cuffed behind our backs.

The police officers asked if they could search my truck and of course I said, "yes." I had nothing to hide. Shortly after that, we were transported to a holding area at the local police station. I'll never forget how it felt being handcuffed to a wall, with one hand dangling above my head, while I listened to the officers talking in the background as they wrote up the report. I listened to one officer joke with his friends, saying, "If that big guy twitched one more time or said one more word, I would've blown his [blankety-blank] head off." I had never been in any real trouble like this before. I had never been arrested before, and I had never been in jail. I sat there in silence and listened as the officer who was in charge of the case stated, "This guy's background check is clean; there's nothing on his record at all."

My mind raced...it was all so surreal, like a dream. Could this really be happening to me? I could barely get my mind around it. Obviously, the next thing that went through my mind was, "God, why is this happening to me?" I'll never forget what the inner voice of the Holy Spirit said to me. He said, "I'm killing your idol." Suddenly, I realized what was really happening—far beyond the particular circumstances at hand. God was dealing with me, and He had allowed me to fall into the hands of the law. And, not just any law. I love police officers. I have good friends who are officers, and I respect the law. But these guys were not like that. Little did I know at that time, I had fallen into the hands of some dishonest men who did not properly represent what the law is really about. In fact, I heard that not too long after this incident, a number of officers from that county were indicted for various crimes they had committed. At the moment, however, none of that mattered. My friend and I were transported to the county jail and put in a large holding cell with a number of others who had been apprehended for various charges. That night in a jail cell was the longest night of my life. In utter embarrassment, I made a call to one of my sons back in Michigan and he had to come and bail me out of jail. The next day was Sunday, and as I took the pulpit that day, it was the hardest sermon I have ever preached. I was exhausted and completely embarrassed by the whole ordeal.

To give a little background to this scenario, my friend and I were on an archery hunting trip in another state. We were hunting a large wooded area on the fringe of a major city. We had discovered that large open areas on the edges of cities were generally overlooked by hunters, even those areas that offered some really good hunting. Furthermore, many of these tracts of land were open for hunting with bow and arrow. We were hunting an area like this when we had our run-in with the law enforcement officers. Not long after we were released on bail, we received several charges, including hunting in an area we weren't supposed to be in. I heard the officers lie to cover up their initial harsh treatment of us by saying they were responding to gunshots in the area, and they thought that we were the offenders. Soon after that, we found out how corrupt the system can be in given areas. In court, I heard officers blatantly lie about the incident with my own ears. Off the record, one of them laughed and said to me that we were toast and that they were really going to work us over.

As I tried to understand what their game was, it occurred to me that they didn't know me from Adam, and certainly didn't have any personal vendetta against either my friend or me. Then it came to me that what they were really after was my truck and all of our equipment, including my properly stored handguns. I had a target pistol and my personal handgun in the vehicle stowed and stored according to the law. Yet I heard an officer lie in open court, saying that my handgun was under my seat with a bullet in the chamber. I had never done anything like that in my whole life. On top of that, I didn't so much as have a pocket knife with me when I was apprehended. I got a lawyer to plead our case. When she heard my story and examined the evidence, she thought the whole case was so ridiculous that she wouldn't take any money from me beyond the initial small deposit that I put down to obtain her services.

After several interstate trips back-and-forth, the judge acquitted me of all hunting-related charges and ordered my equipment returned to me. However, based on the false testimony of the officers, he did charge me with improperly storing my firearms. Even though this was not true, it didn't matter. They took my handguns, and later when I read the report, it was inaccurate and didn't properly represent the weapons that were confiscated. On top of that, when I got my truck back, all the tires were flat and thousands of dollars' worth of our equipment, including my archery gear, had been stolen.

Divine Discipline

During this time, I struggled with some anger and unforgiveness. I fought to forgive the officers who arrested us and lied about me. It was truly a hard thing to do. But I was able to do it. I love those men now, and I pray God's best for them and their families. In spite of the difficulty of going through it, a very positive outcome is that this incident helped me realize the struggles that some people go through when they have been mistreated or abused, and the degree with which they need to commit themselves to actually forgive others. But above and beyond all of that, I realized that God was dealing with me in a very specific, particular way that could not be ignored. Gradually, as I thought about it, I realized that I really had it coming, and that God was using the situation to stop me cold in my tracks in a number of areas. I was under God's divine discipline.

The Word of God talks about being disciplined by God in areas we need to change or grow in. Hebrews 12:5-11 (NIV) states:

And have you completely forgotten this word of encouragement that addresses you as a father addresses his son? It says,

"My son, do not make light of the Lord's discipline, and do not lose heart when he rebukes you, because the Lord disciplines the one he loves, and he chastens everyone he accepts as his son."

Endure hardship as discipline; God is treating you as his children. For what children are not disciplined by their father? If you are not disciplined—and everyone undergoes discipline—then you are not legitimate, not true sons and daughters at all. Moreover, we have all had human fathers who disciplined us and we respected them for it. How much more should we submit to the Father of spirits and live! They disciplined us for a little while as they thought best; but God disciplines us for our good, in order that we may share in his holiness. No discipline seems pleasant at the time, but painful. Later on, however, it produces a harvest of righteousness and peace for those who have been trained by it.

The reason I share these things with you is the fact that I have noticed that many believers just think the devil is after them or that life's circumstances are against them when things go wrong, and they wonder where God is in the whole picture. They wonder why He is letting different things happen in their lives. What many simply don't realize is that they are in a period of divine discipline. The purpose of that discipline is to help us to stay on track with God's divine purpose for us and to grow us up spiritually.

Sometimes discipline can be something like Army Boot Camp. That kind of discipline is not punishment, but rather it is something we all need to go through at some point. This discipline is just meant to toughen us up and develop our character. Just like a training sergeant, God doesn't necessarily make things very easy for us. Sometimes we have to press on and on and on, without obtaining the desired results that we would like to see in our lives and our families. When we find ourselves in a period of time like this, we need to push aside discouragement and the lies of the devil, who is telling us God doesn't care or is ignoring us. We must persevere and hang on until He comes through for us. God takes us on a journey through periods of time and discipline like this, knowing that we will be much better off for it. He knows we will develop patience, endurance, and perseverance. These three words all mean the same thing, but different translations of the Bible use these words interchangeably, and I want us to understand how important it is to develop a godly toughness that sees things through to the end.

Hebrews 10:36 (NLT) says, "Patient endurance is what you need now, so that you will continue to do God's will. Then you will receive all that he has promised."

James 1:4 (AKJV) goes on to say, "But let patience have her perfect work, that you may be perfect and entire, wanting nothing."

That is the end result of what I will call "God's Boot Camp Discipline."

Another Type of Discipline

There is yet another kind of discipline that seems a lot more like punishment than conditioning. Unfortunately for me, that is the kind of discipline I was experiencing in this story. Even though the event I just described happened a long time ago, the lessons I learned are still fresh in my mind. Very slowly, over a period of time, I had gradually let my love for hunting and the great outdoors take too prominent a place in my life and become somewhat of a God to me. I didn't realize it at first, but year after year, the more I pursued my sport, the more and more crazy I became, until it became somewhat of an obsession. I remember lying in bed at night sometimes, finding it hard to sleep as I lay there planning and strategizing the next morning's hunt.

I remember one deer season where the night before opening day there was a huge blizzard, and all the area schools and many of the highways were closed. But that didn't stop me. When I got up at 3 a.m., the temperatures were single-digit and the wind was howling, yet I drove for five and a half hours to get to my hunting site, sometimes with almost zero visibility. I could hardly see the highway. (They actually closed it down while I was on it). At times, I was only going twenty-five or thirty miles an hour and couldn't see where the highway was, but nothing would stop me. I finally arrived at my hunting spot. I went way out into a frozen swamp in the snow and the wind. I climbed high into a tree and sat in that tree all day. I was heavily bundled up in over $500 worth of special winter gear, waiting for that giant deer of a lifetime. But because the weather was so bad, I never saw one animal that whole day. When I climbed out of the tree at dark and went back to my truck, I was so cold and stiff I could hardly walk. I probably had hypothermia as well, but even that didn't discourage me one bit. That was just one of many crazy things I did in the name of hunting.

Looking back at my temporary insanity, I am convinced if I would have prayed and sought God that hard, I could have dramatically improved the growth and effectiveness of our church. Instead, I was temporarily distracted and not putting my best effort into the Kingdom of God. The whole incident I described earlier in this chapter, along with all its pain, inconvenience, and expense, plus wasted time and embarrassment, stopped me cold in my tracks. God hit me where I lived, at the center of my misplaced affection. I must tell you, it really hurt.

During this period of time, I read a story in the Old Testament that seemed to parallel what I was going through. It was about a time when David came under God's divine discipline because of something he had done that displeased the Lord. He had gotten proud of his success as a king and started to find his security in how powerful he had become, and how large his army was. He was warned by his generals and staff not to do a census of his country's population or the size of his army, and that if he did it, he would be doing it to assess his own strength and place his security in that instead of God. David's staff knew it would displease God. But he ignored them and did it anyway. God was displeased and decided to discipline David. He gave David an interesting choice. He said, you can either fall into My hand of judgment, or you can fall into the hands of evil men that are your enemies.

In 2 Samuel 24:14 (NCV) it says, "And David said to Gad, 'I am in great trouble. Let the Lord punish us, because the Lord is very merciful. Don't let my punishment come from human beings.'" David chose to fall into the hands of the Lord and not into the hands of his enemies, who would be merciless. Unfortunately for me, in my case I had fallen into the hands of some people who were merciless and were not interested in treating me fairly. Even though they were wrong in the way they treated me, I looked beyond that to my Heavenly Father, and I knew that I deserved any pain or inconvenience I was incurring. If you get spanked by the God of the universe, He can hit you like no one else. It's like an infliction of divine pain that only seems to damage what needs to be removed and leaves all that is good in place. And for that matter, stronger and better.

During my time of discipline, a song written by Bob Hartman, the founder of the Christian rock group Petra, became my mantra (for lack of a better word). I am convinced that the author of that song must have undergone some experience of divine discipline to be able to pen such powerful words. I am a guitarist myself and when I heard the driving, powerful rhythm followed by the lyrics to that song, it touched me at the center of my being. For a while that song became the ringtone on the phones of my three sons, as well as on mine. The song title is, *Hit you Where you Live*. Here are the words.

You want to change, with all your might
You want to do right in his sight
It's his delight to give you your desire
It's his desire to set your life on fire, on fire

Sometimes it hurts when reprimanded
It hurts him more than it's hurting you
He'll pick you up from where you landed
When he knocks you down, turns your life around
He'll turn your life around

Hit you where you live, you can't hold back
When you're struck by his love you will know
Hit you where you live, it's so close to home
When you're all sold out the mark will show
Let him hit you where you live

The evidence leads to conviction
When we don't live everything we say
There's got to be a crucifixion
We can live dying everyday

You've got to tell him he's free to take a shot
He wants to hit you with everything he's got

Hit you where you live, you can't hold back
When you're struck by his love you will know
Hit you where you live, it's so close to home
When you're all sold out the mark will show
Let him hit you where you live
A lost and dying world is dying to know

He lives the only way they'll know, what he has to give
Is when we're hit where we live

On fire, on fire

(Billy Smiley, John Elefante,
Robert Hartman)

The song ends with a blazing guitar line, mixed with the lead vocalist literally screaming out the words, "on fire." I must say, the end result of being disciplined by God was just that. A blazing fire of passion to embrace and do God's will was rekindled more powerfully than ever before. First came the pain, and a feeling of loss and brokenness. Then, a repentant attitude and a desire to pay attention to what God wanted to teach me. Next, a sense of security in knowing that God loved me and was personally dealing with me, even though it hurt. And finally, a renewed sense of God's presence and a fresh commission to run my race and finish my course.

Several years after this experience, God took my three oldest sons and me through the same disciplinary course again. Sometimes we don't fully learn the lessons God wants to teach us the first time around. We had started hunting in a couple of neighboring states about seven or eight years before and found there were better opportunities there, along with less hunting pressure (hunter density) than in our own state. One of the challenges of hunting another state is that many of the rules are different. Unfortunately, we didn't pay enough attention to the different rules. As a result, we broke some of them and received a handful of citations which resulted in fines, plus the loss of some of our taxidermy mounts. On top of that, we lost our hunting privileges in one of these neighboring states for several years.

The whole ordeal was very embarrassing and hard to go through. It humbled all of us and struck a true deathblow to our misplaced priorities. My sons had proven to be so successful in this type of endeavor that they had been on the verge of starting their own hunting club and launching an outdoor TV show. They had expensive cameras and lots of awesome, exciting bow hunting footage, including some where they were using old-fashioned longbows and traditional archery equipment. But now it was all out the window. As I look back on the whole episode, I realize that perhaps our lives were headed in the wrong direction and that God did not want our emphasis to be in that arena. As a result of God's divine discipline, I made an even stronger decision to put first things first, far more than I had before. In everything that happened, I watched all my sons respond in the right way. Through it all, God has redirected their lives and their priorities as well. Today, I can say that they are all involved in some form of ministry whether it be leading worship, leading men's groups, or heading up mission trips and outreach teams to touch hurting people in our community. We all still love the great outdoors and outdoor sports, but I believe those pursuits are secondary to putting God first in every area of our lives.

I am not proud of the mistakes and failures I've made in the past. I would just as soon forget about them and never talk about them again. But I don't want to only talk about the positive things where I succeeded in life. I also want to humbly share some failures and mistakes too. I learned a lot from them. If we look in the Bible, it does the same thing. It paints the whole picture the way it really is—good and bad. It doesn't go around people's shortcomings or the mistakes that they made. Why? Because I believe there is much to be learned about how to navigate this life in a way that is pleasing to God. My purpose in sharing this story is simply to challenge us all, myself included, to continually examine the way we live our lives.

This world has a lot of distractions for us as believers. It is also full of temptation and pitfalls that could lead us astray and get us off the track of following God's plan for our life. Remember the parable Jesus told to his followers about the farmer who sowed seed on various types of ground? Some of the ground was bad and the seed could never truly take root. Other ground had a lot of potential, but weeds and thistles choked out the good seed so that it could not grow up and bear fruit. Obviously, the seed in the story represents God's Word that grows in our lives and produces fruit as we obey it. Jesus explained the weeds and thorns as things that get in the way of our spiritual growth. In Mark 4:19 (NIV) Jesus says, "But the worries of this life, the deceitfulness of wealth and the desires for other things come in and choke the word, making it unfruitful."

No Other Gods Before *Him*

Sometimes even things that are good in and of themselves—like hobbies or sports—can take up too much of our time and focus. Many people try to get more fulfillment out of these things than these things were meant to give. When we find ourselves doing this, we are trying to fill a hole that only God can fill. Nothing else can do it. Not golf, not NASCAR, not football, basketball, or baseball. Not shopping or clothes or new toys - not food or drink.. Not jobs or career, not sinful habits or addictions, or any other thing not specifically mentioned in this list.

From time to time, if or when I find myself being distracted from my purpose by the love and pursuit of other things, I remember the discipline I received. We really do have a Heavenly Father who wants our love, our affection, and our obedience. He wants to grow us up to be just like Him and follow in His footsteps. And so, just like an earthly father, He personally plans our life and runs us through the paces. He uses both types of the discipline I have shared here to keep us on track. Hebrews 12:9 (NLT) says, "Since we respected our earthly fathers who disciplined us, shouldn't we submit even more to the discipline of the Father of our spirits, and live forever?"

Always remember one thing. Our Heavenly Dad is disciplining us because He loves us so much. *He loves us too much to leave us the way we were.* His discipline is proof of His love. It is proof that we are His sons and daughters. Philippians 2:13 (KJV) says, "For it is God which worketh in you both to will and and to do his good pleasure."

Take Away

As children, receiving healthy discipline and correction was not something we welcomed with open arms. But as we matured, we realized that our parents, teachers, and mentors undoubtedly disciplined and corrected us because they loved us and wanted the very best for us. This couldn't be truer than in our relationship with our heavenly Father. There are seasons where we find ourselves in a period of divine discipline. In this world, there are many opportunities to fall into sin and become distracted as we place the importance of our own interests, desires, and hobbies in front of what should be our first priority—God. This is known as having an idol, and God will often show us the need to illuminate anything that we put in front of Him through His merciful discipline and conviction, which brings something to our attention that needs to change.

Discussion:

1. When you were a child, how were you disciplined? Did you find it fair? Appropriate? Inappropriate?

2. Not all earthly discipline is healthy; how is God's discipline different?

3. How can a good and productive thing like work, a hobby, or other legitimate interests become a bad thing?

4. Discover your idols. Fill in the following blanks and determine if there are things that you put in front of your relationship with God.
    a. I can't live without _____.
    b. When my mind is idle, I think about _____ _____.

    c. The most important thing (or person) in my life is
_____.

    d. I know God wants me to give up_____
_____, but I can't.

Activate Your Faith

- Now that you've identified some key idols in your life, decide to make a change that puts God back into the driver's seat of your life.

- Memorize and ponder the following scripture verses:

  - *"And have you forgotten the encouraging words God spoke to you as his children? He said, 'My child, don't make light of the Lord's discipline, and don't give up when he corrects you. For the Lord disciplines those he loves, and he punishes each one he accepts as his child'"* (Hebrews 12:5-6 NLT).

  - *"But the worries of this life, the deceitfulness of wealth and the desires for other things come in and choke the word, making it unfruitful"* (Mark 4:19 NIV).

  - *"For God is working in you, giving you the desire and the power to do what pleases him"* (Philippians 2:13 NLT).

Chapter 9
The Challenge of Grace

"For the grace of God that brings salvation has appeared to all men, teaching us that denying ungodliness and worldly lust, we should live soberly, righteously, and godly in this present age." (Titus 2:11-12 NKJV)

After all, we are all sinners who have been saved by grace."

These were the words of a married man who had just been confronted with a very serious sin. I challenged him to change his ways. However, he refused to change, and went on to involve another woman in his life and brought damage to two different families. Sadly, because of this fall from God's grace, he ended up leaving the church. The full point of his first statement was something like, "Hey, grace and forgiveness covered all the things I've done wrong up to this point and it's covering everything I'm doing wrong now. After all, we're not perfect; we all need grace on a daily basis."

I bring this story up because it reflects a huge mistake that many people make when they decide to follow Christ. They think grace automatically covers anything they do wrong. They don't realize the true purpose of grace. I remember back when I gave my life to Christ and began to follow Him. For the most part, I changed my sinful lifestyle and found great peace on the inside that only comes from being right with God. However, as I went on I began getting sloppy. I guess I knew I was forgiven and going to heaven and that God's grace covered sin and any other mistakes I made. As time went on though, my conscience began to trouble me. I had this feeling that whenever I repeatedly engaged in wrongdoing in any area, what I was doing was not acceptable to God. I kept confessing these things to God and asking for His forgiveness as the Bible says we should, but more and more, I realized my confessions had a hollow ring to them. God didn't want me to just keep doing the same sinful things He had forgiven me for, no matter how big or small they were. He forgave me and gave me a new start so that I could live the way I was supposed to live *from* the start.

The true purpose of grace is to forgive our past mistakes and give us the power to live a completely different life. God's grace gives us an exit off the highway to hell, onto a new road that leads to eternal life and heaven. God's grace is *not* a license to continue on the same road of willful sin with some form of insurance policy against future consequences and judgment. Yet, for some reason, many people continue to believe that. They walk in willful, sinful patterns using grace as an opiate to their conscience. This has been a recurring problem ever since the good news of the gospel was preached. Apostle Paul addressed the problem of misusing grace in Romans 6:1-4 (NIV) when he said:

What shall we say then? Shall we go on sinning so that grace may increase? By no means! We are those who have died to sin, how can we live in it any longer? Or don't you know that all of us who were baptized into Christ Jesus were baptized into his death? We were therefore buried with him through baptism into death in order that, just as Christ was raised from the dead through the glory of the Father, we too may live a new life. In other words the real purpose of Grace is to forgive us for our past mistakes, and give us a fresh start along with the power to live the life God intends for us to live, doing things his way, obeying his commands and following his will and plan for our life.

The Truth Will Set You Free

I will never forget one of the early lessons I learned as I began to walk in God's grace on a daily basis. When I was a boy, I learned that I could very easily get out of sticky situations by telling a lie. As time went on, I began to use this tactic whenever it was convenient. I didn't become a pathological liar, but it did become a pattern in my life that I had no problem using if or when it worked to my advantage. I knew it wasn't right to lie, but I didn't make that big a deal out of it either. I remember reading the Bible, in the book of Proverbs about some of the things that God hates, and one of them was lying (see Proverbs 6:17 NIV). While I might have had a small dislike for lying, I wasn't really a hater of untruth to the extent that God is as I read in my devotions.

At one point, I specifically looked at that pattern of sin in my life and thought, "That has got to stop." So, I asked God to forgive me for my sins of the past, and help me be totally honest in every situation. However, for a short time after this, I continued to occasionally resort to using lies when they were convenient. At the same time though, I had a growing uneasiness that this was not acceptable to God. I kept asking Him to forgive me and knew deep down in my spirit that God's grace was not just a Band-Aid to cover my sin. His grace was meant to forgive my bad performance while I worked hard to replace it with a godly performance that measured up to His standards.

It all came to a head one day when I was out hunting with a friend of mine who I had led to the Lord. We were walking across the field together and he asked me a question about something very particular that I did not want to answer truthfully. So, I lied. Immediately, the Holy Spirit convicted me in a very powerful way. I heard the inner voice in my conscience say, "You need to stop that." Inside myself, I said, "Yes, I have to stop that. God please forgive me." Then the inner voice said, "Tell your friend what you just did." When that happened, something inside of me exploded; fear gripped me. Instantly, a full-blown war erupted inside me. To lie means to cover the truth and keep things in the dark. The Holy Spirit was telling me to do the exact opposite by bringing it out to the light. At that moment, I knew God was dead serious about me changing and that He was telling me to do something that would strike a deathblow to that habit.

I walked all the way across the field warring with myself, not wanting to do what I knew I had to do. There was no escaping it. I was under Holy Spirit conviction. Yet I was concerned about my image and my relationship with my friend. It would be very embarrassing to tell a young student of the Christian faith who I had led to the Lord that I had just blatantly lied. But I knew I had to, so I just blurted it out and said to him, "I just told you a lie." His response shocked me. He immediately chuckled and said, "I knew that, the minute you opened your mouth." Then he said, "I forgive you." That inner struggle in the middle of a snowy field, along with my clumsy confession, struck a deathblow to the pattern of dishonesty in my life. From then on, I have made it a point to tell the truth. My career in the sales world became an every-day course in learning to be godly in this area. My motto became "A really good salesman can tell the truth and still sell it." As time went on and I became a Bible teacher, ex-pounding on God's truth, I realized that purity and honesty in every area of our life is God's ultimate intent for releasing His grace into our lives. Ultimately, His goal is to make us like Him.

Psalms 51:6 (NIV) states, "Yet you desired faithfulness even in the womb, you taught me wisdom in that secret place."

Grace is so awesome and covers so much sin and dys-functionality that it is easy to misuse and take advantage of. To put it plainly, even if we walk in willful sin for a period of time, the minute we decide to stop sinning, God *will* forgive us and just like that we are right with God again. I think that the very nature of grace is the thing that makes it so easy to abuse. Pretty soon, we start letting down our guard against sin because we know God will forgive us; however, this is a very dangerous way to live. Why? We have a number of deadly enemies that will begin to close in on us the minute we start using grace in the wrong fashion.

First of all, the devil is always watching our lives, looking for an opening to deceive us and lead us astray through temptation, deception, and wrong thinking. Secondly, our old nature (which we are to reckon as dead and powerless) begins to gain strength when we continue to sin. The end result of doing that is we will experience some serious inner conflict between our old and new nature that we would be wise to avoid. Remember that old saying I quoted earlier: "Sin will take you farther than you wanted to go, it will keep you longer than you wanted to stay, and cost you more than you wanted to pay."

The third consequence for abusing grace is that we slowly become deceived as to the real purpose of grace, and we run the risk of developing a hard heart that is not sensitive to the Holy Spirit. Eventually, we find ourselves attempting to use grace to cover a worldly, sinful lifestyle that does not please God. The influence of this fallen world begins to creep back into our lives. Eventually, we develop a mindset that thinks that because we have a relationship with God, everything is alright - including the things that aren't.

A Fall from Grace

There is a very scary verse in the Bible that talks about what happens when we continue to sin willfully without stopping. Hebrews 10:26 (NIV) states, "If we deliberately keep on sinning after we have received knowledge of the truth, no sacrifice for sins is left." In other words, the voice of grace is saying, "I forgave all of your past sins. I am covering all the sins of omission (sins that you aren't even aware you are committing), but what I am not going to do is cover sins that you deliberately continue to commit without any intention of changing."

Again, I want to say God's grace is amazing. He knows the struggle we all have in erasing patterns of sin that have held us for so long. He knows we have moments of weakness where we might drift in and out of sinful patterns. But we must keep turning to God and confessing our sins with every intention of ending every sinful pattern in our lives. 2 Timothy 2:19 (NIV) states, "Nevertheless, God's solid foundation stands firm, sealed with this inscription: 'The Lord knows those who are his,' and, 'Everyone who confesses the name of the Lord must turn away from wickedness.'" In other words, we must stop sinning. We must all travel the path of eliminating every sinful pattern from our lives. If or when we do sin in a moment of weakness, there are wonderful promises in His Word of forgiveness and the promise of ongoing grace working in our lives. 1 John 1:9 (KJV) says, "If we confess our sins, he is faithful and just to forgive us our sins and to cleanse us from all unrighteousness."

John goes on to state two conditions we must meet to be assured that the blood of Christ is cleansing us from sin in an ongoing way. 1 John 1:7 (ESV) says, "But if we walk in the light, as he is in the light, we have fellowship with one another, and the blood of Jesus his Son cleanses us from all sin." This is an amazing promise from God that should bring every believer a lot of security, as well as great direction for their lives. First of all, we must live in the light of everything we know from God's Word. Our conscience must be clean because of an inner sense that we are obeying His Word and seeking to follow the Holy Spirit's leading in our daily lives. When this happens, we have peace inside and a "knowing" that everything is right. Secondly, we must be right with other people. There can be no unforgiveness or offenses that have not been dealt with. We must have clean, open relationships with each other. When these two things happen and we are right with God and others, we can know that Christ's blood is cleansing us now and continually of all sin. It's the only way to live, and the peace and fulfillment that comes from perfect alignment with God is indescribable.

Set Free to Live

There is a short story from the Bible that perfectly gift wraps the two main aspects of grace that we must understand. In a raw and brutal scene, a woman caught in the act of adultery was apprehended and dragged in front of Jesus by a group of men and religious leaders who said, "This woman broke the law God gave to Moses; she must be stoned to death. What do you say?" Up to this point, the Jewish nation had only known about the Law. The Law (the Ten Commandments) was basically given by God to point out right and wrong, along with the penalties for disobeying the Law. Jesus' mission was to introduce grace to a people who only knew about the penalty for disobeying the Law. At the point where this woman was brought to Him, He had been touring throughout the countryside, sharing the new message of grace and telling people they should turn the other cheek, forgive each other, and go the extra mile. This message seemed contradictory to what the Law stated. And now this seeming clash of ideals all came to a head in one intense, emotional moment. It looked like a head-on collision between law and grace.

Jesus did something amazing. He did not contradict the Law of Moses and He did not deny that the woman was facing a legal penalty for her actions. Instead, He challenged the crowd's right to judge. He said, "...He who is without sin among you, let him throw a stone at her first" (John 8:7 NKJV). In doing this, He was pointing out the fact that everyone was guilty of sin and facing penalty. The crowd of men all left sheepishly, one by one, knowing that they were guilty of sin and thereby disqualified to execute the sentence. Then Jesus turned to the poor, shuddering lady on the ground before Him. He asked her, "Where are your accusers?" She answered, "They are all gone, Lord." He then uttered the words that only grace can utter. He said, "...Neither do I condemn you; go and sin no more'" (John 8:11 NKJV).

It was amazing! Instead of consequences, Jesus just let her go. She was *completely* off the hook. Wow! Wow! Wow! Can you imagine the impact on everyone watching? All they had ever known was, if you do wrong, you're in trouble. Now she was free - and so is everyone who ever receives the beautiful forgiveness that grace provides. But, along with that grace comes a challenge and a mandate to us to stop sinning and live the new life that grace provides. We are free because Jesus paid for our sins on the cross. And, we have been freed so we can live the new life God intends for us to live. Grace spurs us on, saying, "Now you are free...go and sin no more."

Take Away

Grace is your "get out of jail free" card. It is through grace that we have been saved and by grace that our sins have been covered. God's amazing grace gives us the power to live a godly life. And while grace covers our future sins that we do not realize we are committing and the relapses back into the sinful patterns of our old self, we cannot abuse and take advantage of the grace— the unmerited favor— that God has gifted us with. We must live out changed lives, because God has given us the grace and power to do so!

Discussion:

1. In our relationships with others, what happens when we extend too much grace?

2. In our relationships with others, what happens when we solely focus on sin, rules, or the Law?

3. How do we strike a balance between grace (from God) and truth (God's Word) as we relate to other people?

4. How does your view of grace impact your ability to receive God's grace? Do you find yourself abusing God's grace? Do you have difficulty receiving God's grace? Why or why not?

Activate Your Faith
- Determine if you have a healthy or unhealthy view of God's grace. If you have an unhealthy view, what must you do to bring yourself back into right alignment with God's Word?

- Memorize and ponder the following scripture verses:

  - *"Nevertheless, God's solid foundation stands firm, sealed with this inscription: 'The Lord knows those who are his,' and, 'Everyone who confesses the name of the Lord must turn away from wickedness'"* (2 Timothy 2:19 NIV).

  - *"But if we walk in the light, as he is in the light, we have fellowship with one another, and the blood of Jesus his Son cleanses us from all sin."* (1 John 1:7 ESV).

  - *"If we confess our sins, he is faithful and just to forgive us our sins and to cleanse us from all unrighteous-ness"* (1 John 1:9 ESV).

- Watch podcast - The Two Aspects of Grace at
  http://rockfordres.org/media/sermons/thetwoaspectsofgrace/

Chapter 10
Who's Number One?

"No one can serve two masters. Either you will hate the one and love the other, or you will be devoted to one and despise the other. You cannot serve both God and money." (Matthew 6:24 (NIV)

I want to share some things with you about money. You might be asking, what does money have to do with my spiritual progress? Well, there is just something about money. It provides the power to get what you want. It can open doors of opportunity and adventure in almost any area. It can be used for our daily needs, and it provides security, along with an endless host of other things. Pink Floyd's famous song "Money," pretty much says it all. It talks about making a stash and grabbing more cash, and climbing our way to the top, while telling everyone else to get out of the way. It talks about greed and the effect money has on people. Just like this indicates, in many cases money seems to amplify the human tendency for self-seeking. If we fall in love with the power and security that money provides, we will have spiritual heart trouble. Well known Irish spiritual leader Jonathan Swift said, "A wise man should have money in his head, but not in his heart."

Money can be used for much good as well, but it is the love of money that causes the problem. If we don't use it wisely and keep it in its proper place, it can become an idol that can damage our faith. 1 Timothy 6:10 (NIV) says, "For the love of money is the root of all kinds of evil. Some people, eager for money, have wandered from the faith and pierced themselves with many griefs." I used to think that this Bible verse was strictly for rich people, but as time went on, I realized it applies to everyone, rich or poor; the temptation to love money and what it can provide over loving and serving God is something we must all address and deal with.

I remember when I was a boy, my parents taught me that I needed to put God first in every area of my life, including money. I would mow the lawn for a dollar, and my mom would not pay me with a dollar bill. She would give me three quarters, two dimes and a nickel. Then she would tell me to put a dime in the offering plate on Sunday. When I got five dollars for my birthday, she made sure that I put two quarters in the offering. When I got a part-time job in high school, she made sure I put 10% of my paycheck in the offering plate in our Sunday worship services. She said it was a way to worship God with our money and keep it in its rightful place, so it didn't become an idol. Sometimes I resented giving the first portion of my money to God. I remember I did it primarily because I was taught that way from my earliest age; however, my heart was not connected to my giving at all. When I got older, I stopped giving that way. It wasn't until a good while later, when I got my heart right with God, that

I began to truly understand what I had been taught about as a boy.

The Bible talks a lot about money and possessions. There are over five hundred verses in the Bible about prayer. There are approximately 500 verses on faith. But, interestingly enough, there are more than two thousand verses in the Bible about money and possessions. Jesus talked about money in sixteen of His thirty-eight parables. In Proverbs 3:9 (GW), God says, "Honor the Lord with your wealth and the first and best part of all your income." I think God's extra amount of emphasis on money and possessions is because they are so closely connected to our heart and our affections. Money seemingly gives us the power to get what we want and what we need. Generally, human nature is self-centered. I've heard the phrase many times that says, "Get all you can, can all you get, and sit on the can." Putting God first by giving [up] our money strips away the self-centered human tendencies that many times control our actions. Instead of staying selfish, we become generous.

All About You

God put us first. He looked on our lost condition and our future judgment. He came down into our lower earth and He waded into our mess. He sent His only Son to show us the right way to live. Then He offered His only Son as a sacrifice in payment for our sins in the most horrible, gruesome death humanity ever invented—a slow, painful death on a cross. Romans 5:8 (NIV) says, "God demonstrates his love for us in this, while we were yet sinners, Christ died for us."

While we were still sinners, doing our own thing, (even before we were ever born), God invested His firstborn Son, the dearest and the best thing He had. Then He gave us His righteousness and a brand-new identity. Our spirits were reborn by the Holy Spirit. He adopted us into His eternal family.

He put us in His will, and promised us an inheritance con-nected to everything He owns. Romans 8:32 (NKJV) says, "He who did not spare His own Son, but delivered Him up for us all, how shall He not with Him also freely give us all things." God made the first move. He proved His love when He gave us the very best thing He had, upfront. He made it all about us. Now it's our turn.

What to Do

Paul tells us what to do in Romans 12:1-3 (NLT):

> And so, dear brothers and sisters, I plead with you to give your bodies to God because of all he has done for you. Let them be a living and holy sacrifice—the kind he will find acceptable. This is truly the way to worship him. Don't copy the behavior and customs of this world, but let God transform you into a new person by changing the way you think. Then you will learn to know God's will for you, which is good and pleasing and perfect.

This is an amazing statement. We literally say "goodbye" to our old lives. We offer God our independence and now we exist for His purpose, first and foremost.

The Money Test

After offering ourselves to God, one of the first things He asks us to do is to put Him first with our income. The pattern for putting God first with our possessions and our income runs throughout the Bible from its earliest beginnings. It was established outside the Law, before the Law and the Ten Commandments even existed. The three patriarchs - Abraham, Isaac, and Jacob - who were the forefathers of modern-day Israel, followed the pattern of putting God first with their possessions. The Bible pattern for giving is called the principle of "firstfruits," which meant giving God your first and your best, before using the rest of your possessions for your own purposes. God established this pattern with Israel after He delivered them from Egypt. In Exodus 13:2 (NIV) God says, "Consecrate to me every firstborn male. The first offspring of every womb among the Israelites belongs to me, whether human or animal."

In Exodus 23:19 (NKJV) we read, "The first of the firstfruits of your land you shall bring into the house of the Lord..." The first portion of our income is called the "tithe." The word "tithe" literally means "tenth." The scriptural principle and pattern for putting God first is giving Him the first tenth of all our income. Proverbs 3:9-10 (NKJV) says, "Honor the Lord with your possessions, and with the firstfruits of all your increase; so your barns will be filled with plenty, and your vats will overflow with new wine."

During the times of the Old Testament, most people were livestock farmers who also raised their own crops to feed their livestock and their families. Wealth and increase was more measured by how much grain they harvested and stored, along with how well their livestock reproduced. Today, increase is more commonly measured by currency. Either way, God established a pattern with the nation of Israel to put Him first with their income and everything they owned.

Putting God first with your income is a big shock to a lot of new believers. It's quite a big thing to start giving the first tenth of everything you make to God. Interestingly enough, what is really going on is God is going into partnership with us. He is including us in everything He is doing. It's like He is saying, "I am bringing you into the family business, and we are going to invest and work together to reap a huge harvest of eternal value." Yet the main thing on God's list is that He is really after our heart. He knows we tend to be selfish and self-centered. He knows that when we deliberately and obediently put Him first with our money and our possessions, it strikes a true deathblow to that self-centered nature. God wants His rightful place of being first in everything that we are and do.

Huge Point

As I said earlier, before God ever asked us to put Him first, He put us first and gave His first and His best upfront. While we were still sinners, before we were even born, He gave His only Son. God told the nation of Israel to dedicate the firstborn male child of every family to Him. But interestingly enough, He followed the pattern Himself and gave His firstborn Son, Jesus, as a sacrifice to pay for our sin. You might say that Jesus was God's tithe and much more. The gift of His only Son was an extravagant, over-the-top offering, and we are all the return on God's investment.

Romans 8:29 (NLT) says, "For God knew his people in advance, and he chose them to become like his Son, so that his Son would be the firstborn among many brothers and sisters." God, in His love for us, gave His only son as an investment and payment for our salvation. Now the return on His investment is millions and millions of brothers and sisters throughout all the ages, redeemed by Christ's blood; now we are children of the Heavenly Father and members of His divine family. So, as you can see, God is not being insensitive or unreasonable when He asks us to put Him first and follow the same pattern He did. When He said, "Give me the first tenth of your income," He is showing us the pathway of love, and when we follow that path, it cuts right across all our priorities. It attacks selfishness and the self-centered nature that used to run our lives.

Interestingly enough, when I gave my life to Christ, giving the tithe was not a big shock, because as I shared earlier, I had been taught from a very young age to put God first with my money. As I look back on it now, I am grateful for having that kind of upbringing. When I gave my heart to God fully and began to follow Him, I returned to the pattern of putting God first with my income. The biblical pattern is to give 10 percent of your income to your local church to support its ministry and outreach, just as Israel gave the tithe to support the Old Testament priestly ministry for God's work. The priestly ministry taught the people how to walk in God's ways so they would reach out to the poor and those in need. They ministered to God in prayer and sacrifice on behalf of the people.

As a pastor, I have found over the years that many people are very touchy about money. One time in particular, we were going to take an offering in our church to meet a very special need that would touch many people's lives. When I started to make the announcement, a young man abruptly stood up and walked out of the church. I found out later it was his first time visiting us and his dad was a new believer who came to Christ in our church. Later he told his father. "That guy is just another typical preacher after our money." It's too bad that there are ministers and organizations in the Christian world who do misuse money and go after people's money in a wrong way. Unfortunately for this young man, he missed an opportunity to get right with God when he allowed an offense in his mind, based on some previous experience in another arena, rob him of the greatest thing that could ever happen to a human being.

Jesus made a very interesting statement about money in one of His messages on giving. It contained both a command and a promise. Matthew 6:19-21 (ESV) says, "Do not lay up for yourselves treasures on earth, where moth and rust destroy and where thieves break in and steal, but lay up for yourselves treasures in heaven, where neither moth nor rust destroys, and where thieves do not break in and steal. For where your treasure is, there your heart will be also." What Jesus was saying is that our money and possessions are connected to our heart, and He was instructing us to send our treasure ahead - pay it forward to God's work -

and your heart will follow. Notice the command to give starts with an act of obedience, but ultimately it changes where our heart and affections lie. Ultimately, a heart change from selfish to selfless is what God is truly after.

The second equally important aspect of giving is that we become partners with God by investing our money in what I call "an eternal portfolio of grace" that helps reach a lost and dying world. The finances that come in through the offerings from our church family carries the good news of the gospel across our city, our state, and across the world. We take care of orphans and widows, feed the poor, and impact our community with good works. Giving is a very important aspect of letting our light shine. Doing all these things costs (what might seem to us like) a lot of money. As we spend it wisely on those things, we find ourselves directly connected in a heavenly investment project that is number one on God's list—saving and helping lost and hurting people. There is no better partnership in the universe.

God wants to use our money to build His kingdom and He promises to bless us when we give. In one rare instance, He literally double-dog-dared the nation of Israel to put Him to the test regarding money and possessions. The nation had not been putting God first by giving Him a tithe of their income. As a result, they were experiencing social troubles, along with drought and famine that had brought great hardship to them. They cried out to God and asked Him for help. God is straightforward with His answer to the people in Malachi 3:8-18 (NIV), "Will a mere mortal rob God? Yet you rob me. But you ask, 'how are we robbing you?' In tithes and offerings. You were under a curse—your whole nation—because you are robbing me. Bring the whole tithe into the storehouse that there may be food in my house. Test me in this," says the Lord Almighty, "and see if I will not throw open the floodgates of heaven, and pour out so much blessing that there will not be room enough to store it" Malachi 3:8-10 (NIV).

I think God offers us the same challenge, along with the same promise of His provision. I think He double-dog-dares us to put Him first. He tells us to test Him. I think He does this because He knows it is really hard to sacrifice our security and our wants, needs, desires, and affections. He knows we are frail and weak in this area, and He wants to reassure us that He's got our back and that He will take care of us. On top of that, He promises to bless us with even more than we need. I have proven these things in my own life, and these principles really work. I have found over a period of time that even though I may have a way to go yet, my heart has slowly but surely been changed from selfish to generous.

Go for It

I'll never forget one of the many experiences I have had in giving. Early on in its existence, our current church was going to construct a building. We had started the church in a school and then we moved to a banquet facility, but we outgrew this space because so many people were getting right with God and then continuing to attend our services. We took an initial offering to kick off the building project. During that week I read the story about the building of the first portable house of worship - called the tabernacle - in the Old Testament. Moses took an offering of materials from the people in order to build it. The people were so generous that they gave more than was needed, and Moses actually told them at some point that they needed to stop giving. As God was blessing our new church family (as well as my own), I felt such a gratitude for what God had done that I wanted to do something over the top like they did in Moses' story. After conferring with my wife - who felt the same way - we decided to put God's house ahead of our own house. We put our house up for sale and sold it. We paid off a small outstanding bill of around $1500, and gave the rest of the money in this special offering for the new church building. I knew I couldn't out give God, so I wasn't concerned that I had nothing left to fall back on. I knew somehow God would provide me with another house as I worked hard and trusted Him.

However, things didn't happen quite the way I expected. Instead of some kind of instantaneous miracle that I expected, I instead got very sick and ended up moving into my mom's house. For a while, things looked pretty bleak, but, that didn't mean God's promises weren't true. I remember thinking "Wow, God! I didn't see this coming. I gave You practically everything I had, and instead of some kind of miraculous provision, I'm sick and living with my widowed mother." I just had not seen things going that way at all. But during the next six or seven months, my life was dramatically marked by God's dealings with me, which ultimately brought dynamic growth in my spiritual life. Sometimes, adverse circumstances cause us to pause and look at how we are living our lives. It was during this period of time that I got a lot more serious about putting God first in every area of my life. I made strong decisions to trust completely in God, no matter what. I decided to be patient and thankful.

The happy end of the story is that in less than a year, my family and I were living in our own dream home, including a 10-acre spread in the country with our own fishpond in the backyard. God miraculously provided the down payment. It was out in the country, in the exact environment I wanted for my young family. It became the dream house for the golden years of our family. When I finally did sell it, I sold it for exactly double what I paid for it — a 100 percent increase!

I have had many miraculous provisions by God over the years as a result of putting Him first. Some of it was just general blessings that come from faithful giving, along with hard work, pay raises, and other things that are somewhat normal. But there have been a number of other times when I have had God blow me away with His miraculous provision.

I challenge you to do what God says. Put Him to the test. Don't worry about what you did or didn't do in the past. Just ask for God's forgiveness, and put the past behind you. Then make a fresh start and follow the biblical principle of giving Him the first tenth of your income.

One of my favorite verses is Luke 6:38 (NLT) which says, "Give and you will receive. Your gift will return to you in full— pressed down, shaken together to make room for more, running over, and poured into your lap." This describes the baskets of the reapers who gleaned the fields. When their baskets got full, the reapers would shake the basket to settle the grain and press it down to make room for more. Then they continued to reap until the basket overflowed. Jesus used this example to explain how God would reward gener- ous giving in a way people could understand. In a very sim- ple way, He explained to them that the amount you give will determine the amount you get back.

Another great verse about giving is 2 Corinthians 9:6 (NIV), "Remember this: Whoever sows sparingly will also reap sparingly, and whoever sows generously will also reap generously." It will take faith, and it can be scary at first. But you will find yourself working in direct partnership with the God of the universe. You'll find that He's going before you, making a way for you. You will know and feel the difference, and you will be paying it forward, investing in eternity, both in your own future and in everyone else you touch in this life.

Take Away:

When we begin a personal relationship with Jesus, we recognize that we are now part of something much bigger than ourselves. We are now in partnership with God to build God's kingdom—that is, to share the message and love of Jesus Christ through giving whenever and wherever it is necessary, so that others may know Him personally as we do. To do this, we must put God first in every area of our life: with our time, talents, money, and our hearts.

Discussion:

1. Why is important to put God first in every area of our life?

2. It can be very difficult to put God first with our money and possessions. Do you struggle to trust God as your provider by offering your "leftovers" instead of your "first fruits" financially? Why or why not?

3. How does putting God first with your finances benefit both you and others spiritually?

Activate Your Faith:

- Test and trust God by giving faithfully the first 10 percent of your income back to God.

- Memorize and ponder the following scripture verses:

  o *"Give and you will receive. Your gift will return to you in full—pressed down, shaken together to make room for more, running over, and poured into your lap. The amount you give will determine the amount you get back"* (Luke 6:38 NLT).

o   *"Remember this, whoever sows sparingly will also reap sparingly, and whoever sows generously will also reap generously"* (2 Corinthians 9:6 NIV).

o   *"Do not store up for yourselves treasures on earth, where moths and vermin destroy, and where thieves break in and steal. But store for yourselves treasures in heaven, where moths and vermin do not destroy, and where thieves do not break in and steal. For where your treasure is, there your heart will be also"* (Matthew 6:19-21 NIV).

Chapter 11
Extravagant

There is one more exciting type of giving that I must share with you. It's something I think every believer who is sold out for God must do at some point in their lives. When they do it, it will mark them for time and eternity. It will dramatically increase the amount of grace that they are able to both receive and give. What I'm talking about is extravagant giving. I believe the level in which we give in every area, including finances, is directly related to the quality of our commitment and dedication to God. It's a heart thing. Extravagant giving is reckless, crazy giving beyond common sense. It is based on love and a total, blown out commitment to God. I am convinced that at some point in life, every believer should do what I am about to share. Maybe even multiple times, and when they do, they will meet God in a very special way.

God originally established 10 percent as a standard pattern and principal for giving in relationship to our income across the board. However, there are times when God may lead us to give extravagantly, far beyond 10 percent. At other times, it may be a decision we make on our own. Either way, God honors extravagant giving with an extravagant response. I remember something that happened along these lines when I was in Bible college. One day, during my morning devotions, I was reading a story about a follower of Jesus named Mary. Jesus had set her free from demonic oppression and completely changed her life. Her heart was overflowing with gratitude towards Him, and she wanted to do something very special for Him. So, she decided to use a jar of spikenard, a very costly perfume that a woman usually saved for her wedding day. It was made from a rare plant found only in the Himalayan Mountains and was imported from Nepal, India to Israel. It was worth tens of thousands of dollars in today's currency. Mary came into the banquet area where Jesus was eating. She poured the expensive perfume all over His feet and then wiped them with tears and her hair. It was a humble, beautiful outpouring of love and total extravagance. She was basically saying, "Jesus, You're everything to me. I'm taking everything that I'm worth, everything I own, including my hopes for the future, and pouring it all out on Your feet." Luke 7:38 (NIV) says, "As she stood behind him at his feet weeping, she began to wet his feet with her tears. Then she wiped them with her hair, kissed them and poured perfume on them."

Some of the religious leaders that were at the feast were very critical of this moment and accused the woman of being wasteful. Even Jesus' disciples were critical of what Mary had done, saying, "That perfume was worth a year's wages. It should've been sold and the money should've been given to the poor." But Jesus had an amazing response to the woman's extravagant act. He said, "Truly I tell you, wherever this gospel is preached throughout the world, what she has done will also be told, in memory of her" Matthew 26:13 (NIV).

Talk about an extravagant return! Think about it. I'm talking right now about her story, which took place over two thousand years ago. I have preached on this story to thousands of people over the years. I am only one of many who, throughout the centuries, have shared this amazing story. It has probably triggered countless selfless outpourings of love, accompanied by extravagant gifts to build God's kingdom. Remember, an extravagant outpouring of giving to God always brings an extravagant response.

A Prized Possession

As I was saying earlier, as I read this devotion as a young student in Bible college, it inspired me immensely. I had been so blessed by God in my early Christian years, and now I was in Bible college. On top of that, I had just met my future wife and gotten engaged. I thought, "What is the most extravagant thing I could do to show my love and gratitude to God?" The only thing I could think of was my most prized possession, an old Brazilian Rosewood D 35 Martin guitar. I loved that guitar. It was a valuable vintage, collectible instrument. To get it, I had traded one of my prized electric guitars to Dana Angle, the well-known lead guitarist of a popular early Christian group called, The Way.

Now, I immediately decided that I needed to give that instrument to someone who really needed it. There was a guy named Mike Chance on our worship team at the time who was quite gifted. He was a young Bible college student just like me, and all he owned was an inexpensive Yamaha guitar. I gave him the guitar as a gift. He was overjoyed, and as much as I loved that instrument, I was overjoyed to give it and never regretted it for a second.

As time passed, that young man went on to become the worship director for Christ for the Nations in Germany. I got married and went back to Michigan, and guess what? Before long, I got a job working in the number one music store in the region. I became the sales manager, working with guitars all the time. I had guitars coming out my ears. Then I joined up with another music store whose owner was a luthier (someone who actually builds stringed instruments). People started giving me guitars. Expensive guitars. We got involved in building guitars for some of the top Christian musicians in the industry and my luthier friend, Del Langejans, built me one and gave it to me as well.

To make a long story short, I ended up selling the business for Del to my friend, Tim Adrianson, who ended up becoming the bass man for our worship band. Since that time, he and his partner built a huge music business named Geartree, consisting of storefronts and online marketing that stretches across the country. I have both the privilege and pleasure to be able to walk into his warehouse or one of his stores and pull instruments off the wall, anything I want borrow. I would grab a special all white or all gold finished instrument for a particular Christmas show or for recording, or anything else I wanted to do. God blessed me so over-the-top in this area - and I can trace it all back to that gift of gratitude that I gave when I was dead broke in Bible college. It truly was the only thing of real value that I owned at the time. But like I said—extravagant gift, extravagant return.

One Final Twist

And God wasn't done with me yet. He had already blessed me beyond most anyone I know in the area of musical instruments and their availability. But He had one more thing up His sleeve.

A few years ago, I reflected on my old D 35 Martin and I thought to myself, "That was a fantastic guitar," and to this day that particular model has remained one of my favorites.

I thought, "I want to add one of those to complete my collection of instruments." I began looking around online and in different stores, just keeping my eyes open for a good used D 35 I could buy. As time went on, I could not find anything I really liked. So, I called up my friend, Tim, and asked if I could buy a brand-new D 35 through his company at dealer cost. He said, "Sure I'll do that for you, but on your way over to the store, stop by my house for a minute." I stopped by his house and he took me inside and handed me a Martin guitar case. I opened it, and I could not believe my eyes. It was an old Martin D 35 - and not just any Martin D 35. It was a special one, called a "Herringbone D 35," with special scalloped bracing that my old Martin did not have. It was exactly what I wanted, and more. It was such a special instrument that his salespeople told him, "Tim you shouldn't put that up for sale. You should put that in the case and put it in your basement and hang onto it." I asked him how much he wanted for it. To my utter amazement, he said, "I want to give it to you as a gift." I was stupefied.

All of a sudden, I realized that this was a God moment. My friend did not know my guitar story. He was just led by God to be very generous. I realized in a moment that God was telling me something very special. He was telling me, "I remember what you did over 35 years ago. I remember your love gift and how you felt about Me, and that's how I feel about you. I am returning your gift to show you My love and care for you, and I'm one-upping you on it." I will forever remember that moment. I realized right then and there that God keeps very specific books and records of all that we do. Nothing is lost or missing. He kept specific track of what I had done, and then at a very specific time, He blessed me in a most extravagant way. I remember determining all the more to be a giver of my time, my energy, my service, my money, anything and everything I could do to build God's kingdom.

I believe God keeps records of more than just money. He keeps records of our service and our good deeds as well. Our church family's ministry and outreach is primarily fueled by the love labor of hundreds of volunteers who give of their time and talents and money. I don't think Christian leaders who are on staff will necessarily get the biggest reward in eternity. I believe that reward will be shared by every believer who does their part to help create an environment for God's grace to touch people's lives. In our church, everyone is important when it comes to creating that environment. From the parking lot attendants to the greeters at the door, to the ushers, to the technology team, from the musicians to the prayer team, nursery and Sunday school workers, the list goes on and on. God keeps track of everything we do and we all share the eternal reward. Listen to what Jesus said in Matthew 10:40-42 (NIV): "Anyone who welcomes you welcomes me, and anyone who welcomes me welcomes the one who sent me. Whoever welcomes a prophet as a prophet will receive a prophet's reward, and whoever welcomes a righteous person as a righteous person will receive a righteous person's reward. And if anyone gives even a cup of cold water to one of these little ones who is my disciple, truly I tell you, that person will not lose their reward."

I believe the true motivation for giving in all areas, including finances, starts with good, old-fashioned obedience when we decide to follow God's Word and His commands to put Him first. But the end result of this obedience produces a transformation from a selfish, self-centered person into someone with a grateful heart and a desire to give. As time goes on, we slowly become more and more generous, motivated by love. We become extravagant givers of grace to everyone around us. In the end, we find that we are not just serving and giving out of obedience alone, but out of a changed heart, motivated by love. This is God's ultimate plan for us—total transformation from the old to the new. It is exciting and motivating to know that everything we do is recorded by God, and all our work effort and our good deeds are being paid forward into an eternal portfolio that will never fade away, but will last forever.

What You Have in Your Hand is Enough

Some people think they don't have much to give. That's a huge lie straight from the enemy. God wants us to give in proportion to what we have. He measures the quality of our giving by that proportion regardless of whether it's very small or some huge amount. A beautiful story in the gospel shows Jesus sitting in the temple, watching people give their tithes and offerings into the moneybox. He watched wealthy people drop bags of coins containing sizable amounts into the box. Then a little widow lady came along and threw just two pennies into the box. It was all she had. Jesus commented on this to His disciples and said, "…Truly I tell you, this poor widow has put more into the treasury than all the others. They all gave out of their wealth; but she, out of her poverty, put in everything—all she had to live on" (Mark 12:43-44 NIV). So there you have it. God looks at the proportion we give related to what we have, not how big or small it is. This goes for talent too, not just money. A story in the book of Acts tells of a lady named Dorcas. She had a sewing skill, and she used to make clothing for the poor and for children who didn't have much. She spread God's love through her sewing, and everybody was talking about it. She was very well-known for good deeds of charity. She simply used what was in her hand to be a blessing. I find it interesting that when she died, everyone mourned her death and they went and told apostle Peter about it. He then took the time to go pray for her, and God raised her from the dead for His glory—her good works could continue. I think this stands as an example to us all. What we have in our hand is important, and we need to use it. It's more than enough to get started. Dorcas stepped into history - she stepped into the pages of

God's Word. God must have thought what she did was very important, and it stands as an example for us never to underestimate or minimize what we have and what we can do.

Above All We Could Ask or Think

I could go on with many more stories of God's extravagant blessing in multiple areas—from family, to church, to finances, and to possessions. When we bought our current church building, we did a pledge drive. A good friend of mine who has the spiritual gift of giving challenged me to pledge a much larger amount of money than what I was planning to give. Earlier on, I told him I wanted him to mentor me and challenge me in the area of my giving, but what he proposed seemed crazy! I even told him so, and his response was, "If you want to pastor a generous, giving church, you have to be generous in giving yourself." At the time, the amount he proposed was almost a full year's salary for me. But, deep down inside, I did have a crazy, reckless desire to go as far out on a limb with God as I could. So I did it, and my wife Caryn and I began to chip away at the pledge, giving everything we cold scratch up towards it. Our plan was to pay it off as quickly as possible, but we figured it would take quite some time to do it.

A year or so later, when we were almost halfway through paying the pledge, something out of the blue happened. A small, local oil company that I had bought some stock in a couple of years before struck oil and then sold out to a bigger company. Much to my shock and surprise, my wife and I started receiving checks in the mail for our investment totaling well over a half a million dollars. I was absolutely floored. I had never seen so much money at one time before. But, far beyond that was my amazement at God's provision and the fact that the promises in His Word concerning every area of our lives are absolutely, positively true. I determined that I was going to shoot the moon with God, not just with money, but in every area of my life, believing for the best, the utmost, the highest, the farthest reaching.

I truly believe most of us don't realize our full capability in Christ. I have humbly reflected back over my life in the telling of the stories I've shared with you. From the time I was empty, lost, and without God, to this present moment. I have the privilege of pastoring a large church with thousands of people who are traveling the narrow road that leads to eternal life. Many times we don't fully realize how much God can do through us. We tend to limit Him, even though He says in His Word, "Now to him who is able to do immeasurably more than all we ask or imagine, according to his power that is at work within us" (Ephesians 3:20 NIV). Just think about it—the divine nature of the eternal God by the Holy Spirit lives inside us. I love the opening lyrics to the song *Limitless* by one of my favorite groups, The Planet Shakers:

> I'm saying goodbye to every limitation. I'm saying hello to the God of my salvation. There are no limits with you, you are limitless, nothing is too hard for you. You're limitless.
>
> (© 2011 Planetshakers Ministries Int. Inc.)

Get off the Sidelines and Into the Game

I have determined to live an extravagant life of going over the top for God and His kingdom with everything I am and everything I own, until my last breath. As I heard an Olympian say recently, "I wanted to bring everything I have to this race, holding back nothing. When it's over I want to leave it all on the field." I challenge you to do the same in your spiritual walk (race) with God. We must remember that whenever God asks us to do something for Him, to give our money and our time, or to serve in any capacity, He is simply including us in what He is doing. God is in the business of saving people, changing them, and lighting up this dark world with the revelation of who He is.

First, He gives us grace and forgiveness. Then comes the mentoring process, where He patiently makes us like Him. In the end, we are CHANGED from lost, self-centered, self-seeking individuals into catalysts of God's grace. Instead of just needing and receiving grace, we *give it* extravagantly in every area of our lives. Over the years, I have read many amazing stories of what God has done through the lives of people who have completely extended themselves and sold out to His purposes. Not only did those stories motivate me, but I felt a growing desire not just to read other people's stories—I want to live in such a way that my life has an exciting, creative, God storyline.

I encourage you to not sit on the sidelines and read other people's stories. Create your own story by "betting the farm" on God. If your steps of faith and commitment to God don't scare you from time to time, you probably haven't extended yourself enough. If you want a crazy, exciting life with a "to die for" storyline, jump into the fast lane. Be extravagant and give yourself first and foremost, and then dedicate everything you own for God's purposes. And don't forget to have moments of reckless generosity like Mary did. Whatever we give from a heart like that, it is never lost. Instead it is preserved, and it takes on real eternal value as we pay it forward into eternity.

I want to highlight a special promise of blessing from a scripture verse that I believe the Holy Spirit wants me to speak over every person who reads this book:

> "And God is able to make all grace abound to you, so that having all sufficiency, in all things, at all times, you may abound in every good work" (2 Corinthians 9:8 ESV).

GOD BLESS YOU. Lay hold of your purpose and your eternal destiny. Run your race, fight the good fight of faith, and if I don't meet you in this life, it is my prayer that I'll see you on the other side.

Take Away

As we discussed in the previous chapter, putting God first in the area of our finances and possessions can be very challenging. At some point in your faith journey, you may decide - or God may lead you - to give up some of your treasured possessions or money toward building up God's kingdom in a specific area. It's exciting, and it can be scary. But the good news is, you can't out give God! He will surely bless you for your extravagant show of love towards Him.

Ultimately, God is not after our money, even though money plays an important role in doing His work. What He is really after is our hearts. He knows that where our treasure is, that's where our heart will be, so He tells us to put Him first in that area, knowing that our heart will follow. This is true about our time and our talents, or anything else of value that we have as well. Matthew 6:21 (NIV) says, "For where your treasure is, there your heart will be also." The end-all is this: we develop an extravagant giving heart just like His. God is love - completely selfless - and He is making us just as He is.

Discussion

1. Have you ever had to give something up that was incredibly valuable to you? What was that like?

2. Could you easily give extravagantly of your possessions or finances if God asked you to? Why or why not?

3. Consider for a moment what Jesus extravagantly gave to you by enduring death on a cross. You are no longer a slave to your own desires or subject to the penalty of sin, and Jesus has shown you His perfect, unfailing love. How do these thoughts affect your view of giving as you seek ways to put God first in every area of your life?

Activate Your Faith

- Pray that God will give you the grace to give with a glad and cheerful heart.

- Ask God to reveal to you the things that you put before your relationship with Him and then ask Him to re-order them appropriately.

- Watch podcast: All In at
  http://rockfordres.org/media/sermons/all-in-part1/

- Memorize and ponder the following scripture verses:

  o *"Now to him who [God] is able to do immeasurably more than all we ask or imagine, according to his power that is at work within us"* (Ephesians 3:30 NIV).

  o *"All the believers were together and had everything in common. They sold property and possessions to give to anyone who had need"* (Acts 2:44-45 NIV).

Chapter 12
Prodigal Grace

In *Changed*, I have described the huge change that came over me when I left my sinful lifestyle and dedicated my life to God. You've heard my story, but now I want you to hear someone else's as well. I want to make absolutely sure that everyone knows and understands that there is no one beyond the reach of God's mercy and forgiveness. No matter who you are or what you have done, you too can be changed.

"Prodigal Grace" is written by my daughter, Carly. I believe when you read her story, any remaining shred of doubt about God's love and His endless mercy will evaporate. If you are feeling hopelessly lost and sinking fast, I believe her story will throw you a lifeline that will connect you to the God who created you. He will turn the light on inside your spirit and give you a new reason to live, accompanied by fresh hope for the future. If you are reading this and you have a family member or friend who has lost their way, it will give you fresh hope and faith to continue to pray for them and reach out to them, because truly, *there is no one outside the reach of God's love*.

Prodigal Grace

Note: In sharing my story, I am not looking to glorify or give undue attention to the things I did, but rather to share my experiences and the *grace* that I was shown. I want to glorify the God who saved me. How extraordinary are those who have never strayed so far and can tell the story of life-long faithfulness. As for me, I deserve no good thing; I chose my way. Yet Jesus saw fit to intervene and change every-thing, with His amazing grace for a sinner.

⁓✕⁓

Last call for drinks...*it's 2 a.m. already?* The music pulsed, the lights swirled. Light-headed and hearted, I crushed out my cigarette, the smoke swirling like the buzz in my head. As my favorite song started to play, I reached over and grabbed her hand, and we laughed our way onto the dance floor. *It's way too early to go home.* I laughed out loud as we moved with the heavy beat of the music. *Why would I want to be anywhere else?* No thoughts of work, no thoughts of depression, no thoughts of regret...no thoughts at all. There was only that moment, that instant.

It was never fun to stick around until the lights came on and the music went off, so we grabbed our stuff and headed for the door, laughing as we headed into the night. No thoughts, no thoughts...

It's way too early to go home...

⚮

While growing up, ours was a happy home, with godly parents who loved and taught my three brothers, little sister, and me. With five kids, our home was never boring, but filled with laughter, love, and all of the other things that make up happy families. We were a fairytale family - in a fairytale setting - until the teenage years arrived. I in particular, (for no particular reason I could understand), increasingly struggled to be out from under my home's shelter. All my life I went to church: Sunday morning, Sunday night, and Wednesday night. I attended a Christian school, youth group on Thursday, and had Christian friends – the whole package. Somehow, though surrounded by the gospel, I now realize that I knew all *about* Jesus, but I didn't genuinely know Him like others around me. I somehow just *assumed* the gospel, taking it for granted.

My first job introduced me to friends who hadn't grown up in the same ways I did. It came as a minor revelation to me that not everyone grew up in church and followed the rules. My first friend at work was named Karen. She was years older than me and, unbeknownst to my parents, introduced me to an entirely new world. First it was different music, then cigarettes, then alcohol, and eventually going out with boys, without any rules. The exhilaration of these discoveries made me fight what I once had seen as the peace and shelter of home. I was an irritable and annoyed brat in general, but most often to my mom and younger sister. Jo-anna was four years younger than me and often wanted to tag along. I would usually brush her off and go on with what-ever I was doing.

There is one memory from this time that still haunts me. One evening, when I was at Karen's apartment after work and thinking about not going home at all that night, my mom - who had begun to suspect some things - called Karen, and I picked up the phone to listen in. She confronted Karen about introducing a younger girl (me) to things that weren't good for her, and the words my mom said that night still bring tears to my eyes: "I would die before letting anything bad happen to Carly." What a young, stupid fool I was, to hold my mother's love so cheaply in order to chase the thrills I was after.

One morning in late October, not long after that conver-sation, we got an early snowfall and mom wanted me to drive to work with my dad that day, since I was only sixteen and the weather could be a hazard to an inexperienced driver. She said this out of love and concern, but I viewed it as getting in the way of what I wanted to do later on in the day. So, I just drove off when she went back into the house.

Just a side note here—over the years as I've told my story, I've been approached by parents who have kids act-ing like I was then, and they ask some variation of this ques-tion: "What goes through a teenager's head that causes them to react in the ways they do?" The only answer I can offer is the explanation of what I felt back then. I was discov-ering this exciting new world and people that enthralled me because I'd never been exposed to anything like it before. Because we grew up in church, attended a private Christian school, and spent most of our time with Christian friends, my parents were able to shelter us from a lot of the things going on in the world. The world outside that perimeter sparked intrigue and my thirst for something more, and an-ything or anyone (even a loving mom) that stood in the way of that triggered a response I didn't even know was in me. And the more I was restricted from this new world, the stronger the desire became. It's kinda' like a kid discovering a shiny, brand new toy, and then having it taken away while everyone wonders why the kid is throwing a fit. Most teenagers are still kids, even though they may appear to be in grownup bodies. Their toys may be different, but their reactions can be the same.

I worked in a little café, and I knew my mom would be coming by that afternoon because she'd be in town and when she was, she always stopped in to say "Hi." I was still mad at her from that morning, so I asked my boss if I could leave early, knowing that then I wouldn't have to see her, and it would also give me a good way to show her how mad I was. My request granted, I left.

That evening, after work, I went to the apartment of one of Karen's friends and did what I'd been looking forward to since that morning...drinking, smoking, and hanging out with some guys I liked. As I headed back home that evening, I kept spraying perfume to try and mask the cigarette smoke and chewed some gum for the alcohol on my breath...

As I pulled into our driveway, there were a couple of black cars parked there, and people in dress suits walked towards me as I got out of the car. The first thought that went through my head was that my older brother must be in trouble for something. They told me that my dad was on his way and to just wait inside the house until my dad got home. So, I went inside and sat with my little brother on the couch. He said he wondered where mom and Joanna were. My mom had left a note on the fridge saying that she and Joanna had taken our dog to the vet and would be home later that afternoon, but so far, they were not there.

My mom always wrote us notes. She put little love notes in the school lunches she made for us every day, wrote letters to friends and family, penned love notes for my dad... she was so good at expressing herself in writing.

When my dad got home and walked through the door, he was accompanied by all the somber looking people in suits. I could tell something major was wrong. He sat down by Daniel and me and gently said, "Guys, Mom and JoJo were killed in a car accident today. They're gone…" The first thought in my head was, *"Don't cry. This is a big joke and they're all gonna laugh at you and say 'Gotcha!'"* But as I looked at my dad and the reality written on his face, I bowed my head as a massive wave of realization flooded over me…and I cried. Body shaking, heaving crying. I cried that day, and I cried into that night until exhaustion finally brought me sleep. When I woke, realization dawned with the morning light, and I cried all over again.

Within an hour after we were told about the accident, our house filled up with loving friends and family. They brought comfort and offered help in any way they could. Over the next few days, my uncle made all the funeral arrangements, meals were cooked…at one point that evening someone asked me to go into my mom and sister's closets and find clothes for them to wear in the caskets. I went along to look and just collapsed with grief among their clothes and belongings, which still carried their familiar scent.

The funeral home visitations were packed. Well over three thousand people showed up to offer comfort and condolences. It was heartening to see the overwhelming number of people who had been touched by their lives.

Between the visitations, I just wanted to get away, so I drove to an apartment a couple of friends were at. As I sat on the couch, one of them brought me a strong drink: whiskey and Coke. It burned as I drank it down, and settled with a warmth that eased - ever so slightly - the harshness of this new reality.

Guilt and shame tore at my soul for the way I had treated my loving mom and sweet little sister. I wrote long letters to each of them, which ended up being soaked in tears, and had someone put them into their hands. I never looked at them in the coffins, which was made easier by the fact that it was a closed-casket funeral. I could have looked at them, but I couldn't bear to.

Somehow, life continued...I had always been a good student, earning a 4.0 GPA, but now I no longer cared about school, so I concentrated instead on friends and partying a lot more than studying. I remember taking an exam where, instead of reading the questions, I just went through and marked random answers. My teacher later came up to me and said, "Carly, I know you're better than this. I'd like to offer you the opportunity to come after school and retake the exam." I turned the offer down.

Karen remained my best friend at this point, and I spent a lot of time at her place while trying to keep up somewhat of a good front at home. She got me a fake ID, so at sixteen, I was going to bars, buying alcohol, and getting into other age-restricted venues. It was a lot of fun when you're a teenager looking for distraction. I experienced many "firsts" during that time, and it only increased my hunger for more.

After my mom died, I had my first serious encounter with what I would later realize was depression. While there are many different causes for depression, of course mine resulted from the emotional trauma of losing my mom and sister so abruptly. To make coping with this even worse than it might have been, the truth was that my mom had done so much for our family. We always knew it, but until she was gone, we hadn't fully realized the all-encompassing reality of all she did. I half-heartedly tried to keep up the housecleaning and other various chores, but I felt weighed down by such a heaviness of heart and mind, with a listless feeling. I had a lack of emotion about pretty much everything. Emotional indifference displaced the pain I felt in my heart. I pushed it down and tried to ignore it because the pain of it was too much. I subconsciously vowed to never hurt like that again, so my heart shut down, my emotions stagnated, and where there used to be the warmth of love and family, a coldness seeped in, numbing me to the point that it was nearly incapacitating.

The only things that weren't overwhelming was anything that distracted me from the pain in my heart: i.e., drinking, parties, music, boys, friends, movies...but anything that required time or effort was like an insurmountable wall.

For those who may not know, depression isn't laziness or "the blues." It is the absence of all feeling, to the point where nothing seems to matter, and even things you know are important seem so overwhelming that just the thought of getting out of the bed and brushing your teeth can be daunting. You force yourself to do even routine things, like a robot. And a robot is what you seem to be from the outside. Depression is a monster. A monster that sucks the life from you before you even begin your day. It's the monster that steals feeling from even the most important things in life like family gatherings and the like. Depression gives the ability to sit and stare at a wall - doing nothing - and feel overwhelmed by all that you know you should be doing, but aren't. It wasn't until years later that I found an explanation and help for this monster, but if you or someone you love is suffering from symptoms like the ones I've described here, please don't wait to seek help. [I've also included some information at the end of this chapter to help steer you in the right direction].

I eventually began a new job as a nurse's aide, and it began a whole new chapter in my life - one that opened many of the doors I had so far avoided. It was here that I made new friends, and we'd meet after work to drink and hang out. I spent more and more time out late, doing rebellious things, until it finally came to the point where my dad gave me an ultimatum of following rules and getting my heart right (offering me his help to do so), or moving out. He couldn't have me living under his roof the way I had been behaving, bringing that bad influence home. And so I moved out.

I still remember the feeling of being alone in my first apartment on that first night. The sadness and lonely longing for my family and all I had known before was mingled with the excited anticipation of what was next, and the possibilities that came with my new, unaccountable independence.

I was as good at my new job as I was with my partying. I earned a reputation of being a quick learner, hard worker, and a responsible caretaker. I really enjoyed my work too, and became especially close to some of the residents in my care.

I cared for patients with early and end-stage Alzheimer's, cancer, dementia, those recovering from surgery or falls, and everything in between. We cared for them all the way through to the time of their passing away or successful rehabilitation. I fondly remember many residents I had the privilege to care for, and am honored to have cared for them.

It seemed, though, that there were two sides of me. On the one hand, I was efficient, hard-working and responsible. I was loved by residents, and appreciated by my bosses and fellow workers. On the other hand, I was a young woman, newly on her own, taking advantage of every opportunity for fun and the fulfillment of things long suppressed.

I lived for the night. Every night after work that I could, I met up with friends to drink, party, flirt, and distract myself from anything I might feel if I stopped.

My job introduced me to many new people, among them some girls I became friends with who opened me to things I had never imagined I would act on. I became good friends with a girl named Amy. We clicked right off the bat and enjoyed working together. We also became friends with another girl named Morgan, who would eventually become a major part of the direction my life would take.

And there was Heidi...where do I start there? From my earliest memories, I thought girls were beautiful, but then, who doesn't? Women *are* beautiful. God created the human body, male and female, magnificently. It's the primary reason why some great sculptures and works of art are so famous and beloved throughout the centuries.

I had crazy crushes on boys, but was drawn to the physical beauty of girls as well—whether it was in catalogs, magazines, or television. It was nothing sexual...I was too young for that. Little girls grow up playing with dolls, Barbie, and dreaming of the magical tales they're told of beautiful princesses' "once upon a time..." Little girls want to be these beautiful girls and find their prince... but not all girls like the prince *and* his princess. Raised in a conservative Christian home, I had no reason or influence to feel that way. But from my earliest memories, I – just - was. Even before I knew it was a "thing," an "issue," a "persuasion," a "choice," a "perversion," a "phase," a "lifestyle," a "right," a...

By the way, I think a strange misconception some people possess is that if someone is gay or bisexual, they must be attracted to a lot of people they meet who are of their same sex, which just isn't the case. It'd be the same as thinking every straight woman is attracted to every man she meets and vice versa. But for some reason, it is sometimes assumed that people with same-sex attraction *surely* must be attracted to or interested in many or even most of their same sex. That is just not true. I've had many attractive friends growing up and throughout the years. You can know someone is good looking without being sexually attracted to them: male or female.

As I said, throughout childhood, to high school and beyond, there were many boys I had crazy crushes on, that kind of heart stopping, can't talk, can't think feeling. Which brings me to the genuine surprise of Heidi, the first time I realized I had a crush on a *girl*...it dawned on me that it was that same nervous anticipation kind of feeling. I'd always been attracted to the physical beauty of girls, but I was surprised by this sudden, emotional commotion.

I was excited every time I saw her name on the work schedule with mine and tried to act nonchalant as we worked together. Despite any feelings I may have had, Heidi had a boyfriend at the time, so nothing developed beyond our work relationship, and it was a couple of years before I saw her again. Morgan, the girl Amy and I had become good friends with, was openly lesbian. One night she invited us to go along with her to a gay bar she frequented. I tried to contain my excitement as I said that I would go out with them.

We spent a lot of time together. Partying, clubbing - all the usual party stuff - but Morgan introduced another aspect to our times together, as she had been involved with the occult. We were interested by some of her stories and played around with the Ouija board, held small séances, and other such things. I remember during séances we would all three hold hands (you weren't supposed to "break the circle") and try invoking spirits to possess and speak through us. There were times Morgan and Amy would completely change under these spells: their voices, mannerisms, and odd stories from supposedly long dead people (demons really) would manifest. One time Amy manifested as a very young, shy little girl, and sometimes there would be violent thrashing with Morgan, with her trying to wrench our hands apart. I don't know what letting go would have done, but it supposedly was very bad, possibly freeing a spirit.

One time, the demon speaking through Morgan looked at me with what I can only describe as an evil, hate-filled, despising glare, and called me "preacher girl," because my dad was a pastor. Her eyes glared into mine with a palpable hate and in a sneering voice said, "I know who you are, preacher girl." This was followed by a guttural sound as her eyes rolled back, and then her body wrenched violently. Every time we held one of these séances, I would feel something like a cold, crawling sensation - like fingers moving up my spine - and I could sense it was something wanting to come into me, but again, what I can only attribute as God's grace, the demonic spirits were never able to enter me. I remember even praying silently as we held these séances, rebuking evil spirits from coming into me. Again, I don't know how all that works; I can only share my experiences with it. Because of this incident, some of our friends gave me the nickname "Preacher Girl."

One night, Amy was going to Morgan's apartment and asked me along. Morgan's sister, Melanie, who was also a lesbian, was there. She was flirtatious and fun, and we all decided to go out one weekend.

One of these nights when we were all hanging out together, I had to get something from my car and Melanie said she'd come with me. We walked outside in the dimly lit drive, and she kissed me. It was everything I'd been waiting for... after that, we became a casual couple; that is, until Melanie eventually moved in with me...and so began some of the most fun, exciting days I'd had yet.

I don't want to romanticize these days or my choices, but as far as worldly fun goes, it really was fun. Parties, hanging out, road trips...I understand why, apart from a true realization of and true relationship with Jesus Christ, people live, love, delight in, and fight for their lifestyle and choices. Heterosexual, homosexual, - whatever you are, whatever you like to do, everyone knows there is both pleasure and happiness to be found in this world; however, I've found it doesn't offer the eternal fulfillment and purpose found in a genuine relationship with Jesus Christ. This world and everything in it just doesn't last.

To acknowledge that people in this world can find a worldly happiness and fulfillment apart from Christ isn't any endorsement or approval of what they do— just a fact of reality. The world can be miserable, but it can also be fun. Many people in many ways are very happy and find temporary, worldly joy apart from Christ. My point is that I understand that and lived it. But in it all, an emptiness that lingered in the back of my mind and whispered its presence through-out those days. Human beings are spiritual, whether or not we acknowledge it.

Regardless, I enjoyed those days. I smothered any conviction from my Christian upbringing and embraced my wonderfully new experiences with open arms and unabashed happiness. Finally, my thoughts, desires, and experiences clicked. As far as that sense of unfulfillment that whispered at night or even randomly during the day? I just tucked it away and distracted myself with whatever was at hand.

One night, we were all out at the bar and it was last call for drinks. Last call for drinks...*It's 2 a.m. already?* The music pulsed, the lights swirled. Light-headed and hearted, I crushed out my cigarette, the smoke swirling like the buzz in my head. As my favorite song started to play, I reached over and grabbed Melanie's hand, and we laughed our way onto the dance floor. *It's way too early to go home.* I laughed out loud as we moved with the heavy beat of the music. *Why would I want to be anywhere else?* No thoughts of work, no thoughts of depression, no thoughts of regret...no thoughts at all. There was only that moment, that instant.

It was never fun to stick around until the lights came on and the music went off, so we grabbed our stuff and headed for the door, laughing as we headed into the night. No thoughts, no thoughts...

*It's way too early to go home...*and so we didn't.

We all went to a house party and then continued with our own party back at one of our apartments. Party, party, party. They all run together, from clubs and hot tubs, to basements and bars. You'd think it'd get old, but it never seemed to at the time. I got to the point of drinking about a pint of whiskey most every night and up to a fifth on the weekend. It was such a regular habit that the clerk at the liquor store would have the bottle waiting on the counter after seeing me walk in. I lived for the next party. I worked hard during the day, so

I could have a good time later, sometimes staying up until 6 a.m. and then getting back just in time to get to work by 7.

It was on a night just like this that we left the same bar, headed to a party somewhere. This time, we ended up in a very rough part of the city. I was driving, and we were trying to navigate out of the area (this was before the time of cell-phone GPS), but we ended up on a road that dead-ended at a big, abandoned lodge that was packed with cars jammed up in every space available.

There was a group of rough looking guys sitting on the steps leading into the lodge, and as our car pulled up to a stop, with nowhere to go, one of the men made eye contact with me and instantly stopped talking, his eyes boring into mine with a look of steel.

He jumped up, eyes still locked on mine, and quickly disappeared inside. Morgan, who was familiar with the reputation of that area of town, leaned over in a chillingly quiet voice and said, "They're gonna kill us." Time slowed to a halt and the next moments are a blur. We had to get out of there, fast. Like some scene from a movie, I kicked the car into reverse and backed up in the only direction there was, toward a narrow opening that would enable us to turn around. Just as I reversed, a car shot in towards us. Had it been even a split second later, it would have blocked us in, with no escape. I tore out of there, squealing around corners and dark streets until we arrived back in the noise and light of the city.

Later that morning, back in the safety of my apartment, my phone rang. As I answered it - before I even said, "Hello" - I heard my dad say, "Carly! What in the world were you doing at 2:30 this morning?" I stopped cold and in a hoarse voice asked, "*What?*" and he repeated, "2:30 this morning: where... were... you?" He went on to tell me he'd been jolted awake from deep sleep at 2:30 a.m. by the Holy Spirit and he woke, saying, "Satan, you can't have my daughter!" I held the phone, listening in stunned silence, with no ready response. I don't know why I didn't fall on my knees and get my heart right with God then and there. This only reminds me how deeply sin will deceive you. I should've fallen on my knees in thankfulness, because in the days that followed, news about this gang came through the grapevine to the effect that three outsiders had shown up on *their* turf, and they would've "tore those girls up" if they hadn't gotten away.

Time passed, and a year or so later, things with Melanie started to fizzle. We never communicated on a deep level. Things got rocky, the fun ran out, and she moved out. I could've tried to stop her, but I didn't. My heart felt suffocated when the door closed behind her. The emptiness and loneliness that before had been a whisper that I'd been able to ignore, now became a flood to the point where I cried out for a long time, experiencing feelings I'd been able to avoid for so long. In response, I hardened myself even more and pushed emotion away. I was hurt and devastated, though you'd never know it to look at me.

During this same period of time, I began noticing how frequently a resident at the nursing home passed away and I did the post-mortem care. One of these times I was training a new girl, and as we started the process, she started to cry and couldn't handle it. I told her she could go take a break and that I would take care of everything. As she left the room, I wondered at the lack of feeling I had and why I never really cried about things, but decided I was just doing my job. I'd cried enough after my mom and sister's accident to last a lifetime.

In the background all this time, my spirit somehow knew that all I was doing was fleeting and empty, yet I pursued it anyway. Pursued it, got it, lived it, lost it - and pursued it all over again. Always searching, always wanting, always hoping to silence that haunting emptiness that whispered. Whether I was alone at night trying to drift off to sleep or having fun at a party, that emptiness would rear its head un-announced. It's a strange thing to be physically intoxicated, yet mentally sober, but that's the state I frequently found myself in.

Throughout these years, some of my friends were in-volved in dealing drugs. I smoked pot once in a while, but cocaine proved to be my favorite. I didn't use it to the point of full-on addiction, maybe holding back because I had known people who were so addicted, they'd forget to eat and hardly sleep at night. I still remember a dealer friend staying over at my apartment and laying out line after line of coke for each of us to have throughout the night. I looked at it on my kitchen counter, laid out so enticingly and somehow decided not to touch it. I can only attribute this decision to the grace of God, that even in my darkness, and as much as I liked it, I never touched the stuff again after that.

In the time that followed, I had another relationship with a girl and some casual flings afterwards. Things never lasted long, mainly because I always kept an emotional distance. It was around this time, while out drinking with friends, I saw Heidi again. She was with a girl, and we found out she was bisexual. I had to laugh at the irony of the situation.

One night I was out at a bar with friends and knowing I had to drive home that night, I stopped drinking long before we left. I felt fine, but was pulled over on the highway for speeding. I passed the coordination tests that I was put through, but the officer also asked me to take a breathalyzer test, which I readily agreed to. Well, I blew a BAC a little over the legal limit and was arrested for DUI. One very uncom-fortable night and a soggy bologna sandwich later, I was sentenced to pay a fine. Some months later I got *another* DUI, but this time landed in jail and lost my license. Unbe-knownst to me, my dad had been praying for me that exact night I was arrested. He was asking God to do whatever it took to get my attention. Thanks, Pa.

Throughout all these years, my dad had always been there for me, praying and making a point to meet me for lunch almost weekly. He didn't cast me off in disappointment or see me as a hopeless case. Instead, he loved me as his little girl. I remember the feeling of being led away from my dad in that courtroom to be arrested and put in jail. One of my biggest regrets is the pain I caused my dad. I caused him to worry so much about me over the years, as well as having to watch his little girl being led away to jail. What foolishness. I'll never fully know how much pain my quest for fun caused.

As I was waiting in a room to be transported from the courthouse to the jail, I saw a policeman glance at me through the window and realized it was a guy I'd gone to school with and had known for years. It served as an embarrassing, shaming reminder of where I'd come from and where I was. The shame continued as I arrived at jail and had to strip and shower in front of a female guard before being led to my cot in general population. After just a week or so, I was called up before the judge, who asked if I'd learned my lesson or if I wanted to spend the rest of the year in jail, thinking about it. I told him I had learned my lesson. My dad was out of town, so my grandma picked me up after I was released. I had never thought that my grandma would pick me up at jail. The shame just seemed to keep getting deeper and deeper.

I went back to my apartment, now unable to drive and suddenly, all of the partying and hanging out lessened. I remember one night in particular, where everyone was going out, but since I couldn't drive, I ended up sitting alone all night at home, dressed up, with nowhere to go. It occurred to me then that people can be your friends when you're useful or have something that can benefit them. But if it's based on having a good time, when you can no longer be a part of bringing that good time as you used to, well, you might find yourself sitting at home.

It was during this time, being grounded as it were, that I was finally forced into self-reflection. The life I'd lived all those years was drifting away, and as much as I wanted to, I couldn't get back to the way things were. People change, circumstances change, life moves on - and as hard as you may want something, nothing stops the inevitability of change.

For years now, I had sensed "other-worldly" things. Voices waking me in the middle of the night, strange sensations, and occasional moments of pure terror. "Demonic" is the right label for it, and I always knew that's what it was. I remember being so freaked out sometimes that I would have videos of a Christian preacher playing on TV and fall asleep to his voice speaking truth from the Word of God, because it calmed and pushed back the darkness I felt. It was crazy and foolish how I could know that God's truth and Word brought peace when I needed to get to sleep, yet I ran from it in every aspect of my everyday life, as though I could somehow drown out truth with the distraction of entertainments.

With the exception of my freaked-out nights where a Christian preacher lulled me into unconsciousness, I used to go to sleep with a heavy metal station playing on the radio through speakers right near my head. All night long those lyrics and sounds affected my subconscious mind and I *know* that it contributed to my darkness and manifested in my attitude and acts of rebellion.

I also used to be enamored with a popular series of vampire books, and just the topic in general. These were my absolute favorites, and the darkness in them fascinated me. I simply devoured any number of books that had titles referencing Satan and other demonic beings, and which portrayed these characters as the heroes. At one point, my dad got a sense of something wrong (Holy Spirit led, I know) and discovered those books in my room. He burned them -

that's how deeply his spirit recoiled against that darkness. Just throwing them away wasn't good enough.

On top of the music and books, I watched certain movies and looked at stuff online that only fed the evil. Weird things would happen to me, especially at night. I would hear voices so distinct that I'd wake up. (One time it was seemingly my deceased mom's voice, which really freaked me out). I would feel strange flutters in the air, as if something was moving by and around me. I was pinned to the bed a couple times, and found that only saying the name of Jesus would release me. (Isn't it strange how I could have faith that that would work in spite of how I was living? This shows the power in His name!) I'm still not sure how that all worked, but I'm not going to argue the point.

Obviously, most people don't read/listen/do all the dark stuff I did, but there are still so many things we naively expose ourselves and our families to by allowing these messages into our home. A book doesn't have to have the devil's name in the title to give an open door to the devil. A song doesn't have to openly glorify the devil to still invite him in.

I think it is important to understand and acknowledge that *parents can do everything right or everything wrong*, and their kids can still go the opposite way. *Christian parents can't save their kids*, but they sure can pray. Even when parents do everything right - like I believe my parents did - still...only God can save. Raising children well is important, and yet, life happens, sin happens, rebellious kids can happen. My dad probably wore himself out with all his prayer for his kids, but he was definitely using the most powerful approach, whether or not he saw the evidence of it at the time. God is the only one with the power to change a life, change a mind, change a heart.

One of these many seemingly endless nights of restlessness, I found myself especially burdened. It seemed that every emotional pain and weight came upon me, wave upon wave. For a time, I had been good at keeping it at bay at night, but, now, this night, it was unavoidable. There was no mental trick, no drink, no relationship, nothing powerful enough to distract or make it feel better. I clearly felt the rawness of pain that I had buried and ignored for so long. Though it had been buried, it stunk. Though it had been avoided, it was a giant. Though it had been laughed at (by me), *it* was the joker. I had no license or car to go anywhere, no friends to pick me up. It was the middle of the night, and there was no escaping my own thoughts and feelings.

Memories played over in my mind, each one hurting worse than the last: happy years growing up; fighting with my mom; leaving work early that afternoon years ago so I wouldn't have to see her because I was angry at her; depression, denial, parties, - all that I had thought would bring joy.

I found myself lying on the floor, curled up, twenty-four years old and yet gripping a little stuffed bear that my parents had gotten me as a baby, a small connection to all the happiness I'd known before the pain came. I literally crawled across the floor to the radio, under such a weight of emotional pain. I tuned the radio to a Christian station and just laid there, curled up in front of it. Song after song played that seemed to be speaking straight to me, I prayed/cried or whispered *"God, if You're real, please come save me, because I don't want to live like this anymore,"* and instantaneously a peace came flooding over me, cutting through the walls I'd built, shredding all defenses, as grace *exploded* in my heart.

The closest feeling I ever had to this one came when I was just a little girl and my parents went out one evening for a date night. My mom had on this floor-length red coat that looked beautiful against her dark hair. It was a wintery night, and when they came home, I was in bed and heard the car pull up as the headlights momentarily lit the room. I slipped out of bed and ran out of my room and into my mother's arms as she walked through the door. I can still remember the white snowflakes on her bright red coat. Her look of surprise that I was awake when I should have been asleep quickly turned to joy as she was holding her daughter in her arms. On my part, that feeling of security and love, that everything is going to be okay and you're safe, that I felt as she held me that night...multiply that by a million, a *trillion*... that's the only picture I can think of that comes close to describing the overwhelming peace I felt flooding into me after that simple but sincere prayer to God.

It was sometime after this night of salvation that I was told about an experience my mom had shortly before her death. She had been praying at church and actually came up to the front for prayer at the end of service. What she'd been praying for was me, concerned about the road I seemed to be heading down, at a loss of what more to do. At the end of that service, she told a friend she'd heard from God that "Carly's going to be okay," and she felt peace for the first time concerning her rebellious daughter. It is amazing how God's peace that ministered to my praying mother years before had now washed over my own completely undeserving soul.

That night I fell asleep in peace for the first time in a long while. How amazing was God's grace and forgiveness. What a priceless gift of salvation.

After this night, everything seems to be somewhat of a blur. My dad and stepmom, Caryn, do more for me now (as well as in all the years before) than I could ever thank them for. I gave notice at work. After staying with dad and Caryn for a time, they made it possible for me to stay in the home of another godly couple who I could also never thank enough for taking me in. While I shared each of their homes, they shared their wisdom. They provided structure and boundaries, where before I'd thrown off all restriction. My dad and stepmom had prayed for years and continued in giving me much undeserved love and help. It was such a comfort to have a secure place to come back to these days. Amidst the changes and all I was learning, they were a steady source of love and grace. A true picture of our Father God's love.

"You're shining!" "You glow!" people said of me when I came into true relationship with my God, who so amazingly saved me. I had chosen my way, but He, my Savior, intervened. I consumed the Bible, Bible teaching, church services, and worship music. I'd sit in my apartment, a Bible in one hand and cigarette in the other, fascinated by these truths I'd heard all my life but only now were my eyes opened, like a veil coming off - to beautiful, awe inspiring, saving truth. I read the Bible every chance I got, told everyone I met about what God had done in my life, and printed out a short testimony that I handed to people I met in passing.

I was able to get a new job in a new city, and move into a new apartment. I recall the joy I exhibited during that time, without even trying. I enjoyed the anticipation of something as simple as reading scripture during lunch break. It was such a strange but wonderful feeling of displacement and new beginnings.

My new apartment was on the top floor, and though it was not fancy, I couldn't have been more thrilled at my new place. It was just me. No roommates, rowdy friends, or even a driver's license to provide distraction. It is amazing how God's grace works. Since I had no license and had completely separated from old friends, aside from walking to my new job, I couldn't go anywhere. I *know* that if I'd had a license, at some point I would have driven back to my old city, bored or reminiscing, to meet up with old friends and take up old habits, straying from the grace of this new life that had been given to me. Thank you, Lord, for working all things to our good. *I'll never truly know what the frustration of having my driver's license taken away saved me from.* Thank you, Lord.

So, alone and grounded in my apartment, I developed a relationship with the Jesus I'd heard about all my life but had taken for granted. He went from being a character in stories I'd heard of growing up and someone I'd heard others talk about, to being someone I anticipated being alone with. I soaked up Bible teaching on TV, worshipped wholeheartedly to music, and even found myself dancing around my small apartment! I glowed from my newfound joy in relationship with God.

I started attending the church my dad pastors, where multiple people told me, "Your dad always said you'd end up here; he just didn't know how long it would take." Not only was I here physically, but I was present in a way I had never been before. I remember attending church, during my period of rebellion, and standing in the back, watching everyone worship, feeling an arrogant, even demonic mockery as I watched them. "These Christians look so silly worshipping God." Now here I was, worshipping my amazing God, with hands in the air and tears in my eyes.

During this time, I had the opportunity to go on an international missionary trip to Poland with a team from my dad's church – and I went. I'd never been out of the country before. I remember the wonderment of being in a foreign place for the first time. All the signs were in a different language, the words and music on the radio and TV sounded strange, and all the conversations surrounding me amidst the din of the city were a foreign, though melodic sound. Our team went to schools, orphanages, and juvenile facilities. I went to a girl's juvenile facility, where I was given the opportunity to share my story. The night ended with girls embracing me in tears as our team prayed for them. Oh, how God's grace translates through all barriers of natural understanding.

I especially remember a school where we ministered. Just before going into one of the classrooms, the administrator told us she'd be surprised to see one particular girl in the class. This girl had apparently been struggling and was rumored to have spoken of suicide. I had the opportunity to share how Jesus had changed my life. As the class ended shortly thereafter, a frail, pretty young girl shyly approached our group. It turns out that she was the young girl the administrator had mentioned. This sweet girl's name was Marzena, and she poured her heart out, telling her story through many tears. She and her friend had been offered modeling jobs, and her friend ultimately died of anorexia as a result of pursuing their career. We cried with her and shared the simple truth of God's love and grace. Our team held a big concert which served as the culmination of our time in Poland, where everyone we had met and ministered to was invited to join us at the end of the week. Marzena came, along with her brother, and both prayed to know Jesus as their Savior.

Our team leaders were from One Hope International. As the trip came to an end, they let me know of an opportunity to intern with the ministry, and I was definitely going to at least consider it, based on the fulfilling trip I had just completed.

After I returned home from this wonderful time of learning, sharing and personal growth, Melanie showed up at my door one night. She'd found out where I lived, and despite all I had experienced and changes I'd been through, I let her in.

One night in particular, we were on the patio, music we used to listen to together drifted out from inside, and we sat there, drinking and talking. In my mind, I thought about and briefly replayed all the fun times of the last years (consciously disregarding all the bad times of those years). There is a blinding allure in the "now" temptation. All I wanted at that moment was something from my past. Forget the emptiness it had held: forget depression; forget loneliness; forget God's grace meeting me on the floor that night not very long ago. There is a ridiculous shortsightedness with desire, which makes a decision in a hasty moment of feeling, acting against the sober wisdom of experience and grace that has been given. In that moment, I felt I could've run away from everything with her. I *wanted* to. I found myself torn inside between my new life in Jesus and the desires of the past. I'm ashamed to say that I was too weak to resist.

She was all I wanted – again - in those moments and days, regardless of all I had been rescued from. I selfishly wanted what I wanted, and took it. After a short time of this, though, I came to myself. Again, this was due to God's grace and the conviction of the Holy Spirit. His patience and faithfulness are beyond comprehension. As I again turned to God in repentance, pleading for His forgiveness and help, He was right there, waiting for me with open arms, like the father in the Bible story of the prodigal son.

Not too long after this, I finally confronted the direction my future would take. I had been praying about whether or not to pursue a missionary internship with One Hope International. I remember getting ready for work one morning and suddenly, clear as a bell, hearing in my mind the words, "The internship. Do it," accompanied with the feeling of absolute certainty that it would be the right thing to do. Whoa! *Only God will interrupt the mundane with the divine.*

So began a whirlwind five years of international ministry in 25 countries. This was the greatest experience I'd ever had, with the greatest people I had ever met. Our team was on fire with passion for the God who saved me, traveling across the globe to speak with people we had never met, and telling them of this God I now truly knew. Living out of a duffel bag, hot, sweaty, hungry, and tired, I felt more alive than I ever had before. My travels with One Hope International taught me that though not everyone has the same life struggles (i.e.; drugs, depression, sexuality, etc.), *everyone* has experienced pain, anger, sadness, hopelessness, and the other human emotions, and all of our struggles have the same answer: a true realization of and relationship with Jesus Christ.

We traveled from Ukrainian orphanages to Ugandan villages that had never before seen white people, to rolling our truck into a river in Mozambique, to the poverty of Haiti and abandoned minefields in Angola. We ventured from the pristine Japan and sensory overload of India, to riding a raft down the mighty Nile river. We experienced the flooding rains of Costa Rican jungles, gangs on the streets of England, and afternoon tea in Romania. It was a wild, roller-coaster ride of adventure that I never would have or could have anticipated, especially when compared to the much different days of my past. I had been pursuing what I thought was happiness and fulfillment, but now what a difference I could see! Oh the goodness of serving God, who lets you in on what He is doing. He is certainly at work, changing people's hearts and lives all across this great big world we live in.

Right near the end of these years, depression unexpectedly reared its horrible head again. I was in El Salvador, doing work with a team of three other girls, and ended up so overtaken by depression that I called a team leader back in the states and in tears expressed my problem and the frustration it was causing to so unexpectedly show up and nearly paralyze me. I came back to the states early and went back home to Michigan. I was able to see a great doctor, who was also a Christian, and he explained that after an emotional trauma (in my case my mom and sister's accident) the 'feel-good' chemicals in people's brains respond by dropping, but that as time goes on those chemicals naturally rise, restoring the previous, normal chemical balance. In my case, after the accident I started drinking and doing some drugs (acting as depressants) which kept my levels suppressed for so many years that I essentially, as he described it, "broke my brain." He compared it to how the body of a diabetic is physically unable to regulate insulin anymore. He prescribed an antidepressant, which helped tremendously. I remember coming upstairs one morning, again lighthearted and unconsciously smiling; my dad and stepmom stopped cold whatever they were doing and stared at me in wonder. It made me realize just how low and dark depression manifests itself.

In spite of needing to leave the field early on my last trip, I stayed involved with One Hope International, occasionally leading mission teams. One of the trips I made was to Peru. Once in Peru, I met the team I'd be working with, and one team member in particular stood out to me from the first moment I saw him. I walked into the room and like some movie, our eyes met and we held each other's gaze. I remember that he leaned back in his chair, resting his hands up behind his head, wearing a big smile that I couldn't get out of my head. For the next ten days, we worked alongside each other, ministering, sharing our testimonies at schools, loading boxes of books, doing anything that the team needed. When the day's work was done, we would go to one of the restaurants or the coffee place right near the hotel. We laughed, shared stories, and probably fell in love before we were ever aware of it.

The day came for the team to go home, and as the rest of the crew was being dropped off at the airport, I went in with them to see everybody off. Ed was one of the last people I saw as he was heading to his gate. At the last possible moment, he handed me a small envelope. The note inside read, "Joy unshared is half joy...sorrow shared is half sorrow." I smiled, looked once more into those eyes, and started walking back towards the airport exit. Just as I was getting far enough away to perhaps be nearly out of sight, I paused slightly and looked back over my shoulder to see him one more time. And again, like a story only God could write, there he was, standing there, looking back at me as our eyes met one last time. I was surprised at the depth of my feelings and the fluttering of my heart as I looked at him. And that was it; we went our separate ways and life's routine kicked back in.

One day shortly after that, there was a phone call for me and I thrilled to hear that familiar voice on the other end of the line. He was headed to Africa for a month and while he was gone, we emailed back and forth, novel-length emails, falling hopelessly in love.

We were married in a small white church in Rockford, Michigan. There was a blizzard going on outside that made everything white. My dad performed the ceremony with a big smile on his face. My husband, Ed, is the most genuine, thoughtful, talented, tattooed, giving, masculine, funny, godly, amazing man. He is my greatest blessing outside of salvation, more than I ever could have imagined. God's abundance is absolutely overwhelming.

❧∞❧

I haven't written my story as some mature Christian who has worked past all her problems. To the contrary, as I've dwelt on my past in writing this, the more I despise who I was, and who I'd become in my heart, and the more I am absolutely *amazed* that Jesus would save me. But that is who He is, amazing and overwhelming in His love. It's the gospel! The Bible is so real when you read that, "For while we were still weak, at the right time Christ died for the ungodly. For one will scarcely die for a righteous person— though perhaps for a good person one would dare even to die— *but God shows his love for us in that while we were still sinners, Christ died for us"* (Romans 5:6-8 ESV).

Throughout the years, I'd heard the "Sinner's Prayer" recited at churches and it always started out "Jesus, I love You and I'm sorry for my sin..." But I didn't cry out to Jesus because I *loved* him, I cried to Him out of my sin and need. I cried out to Him from my own undoing. And, despite of all the ways I had lived as an *enemy* to His love, His grace didn't for a moment hesitate, but rather *rushed* to meet me on that floor. *That's* who Jesus is; *that* is the Jesus who comes alive in the pages of the Bible. I was spiritually dead, Jesus made me spiritually alive "...And you were dead in the trespasses and sins in which you once walked, following the course of this world" (Ephesians 2:1 ESV).

I grew up hearing all about that Jesus and assumed that I knew Him because I knew so much about Him. I had no idea. It is only in encountering the living Jesus Christ that you can even begin to comprehend so great a salvation.

I called to Jesus out of my desperate emotional and spiritual need, but have since been on an intellectual journey as well. I love research and have looked into the things that made me doubt Christianity (though I grew up with it) and arguments against the reality of God and Jesus. After much debate and years of personal doubt, I've found that the Christian worldview offers valid and understandable answers to the questions raised against it. While my story is very emotional, I'm not sharing my story to play on emotions. Instead, my theme is that Jesus is the all-encompassing answer to life on this earth and through eternity. (For your own reference, consider reading the writings of Ravi Zacharias and C.S. Lewis, though there are so many others as well).

Old issues creep up unexpectedly even years later and new things I wasn't aware of surface: new joys, new discouragements. This is the way life goes, but we don't have to stay the same doing the same things. We can receive forgiveness for our sins and face life with Jesus, or try and push through on our own. I know by personal experience where the latter ends up: in heartbreak, numbness, or indifferent happiness and unfulfillment. I lived for years "... having no hope and without God in the world. But now in Christ Jesus, you who once were far off have been brought near by the blood of Christ" (Ephesians 2:12-13 ESV). And, thank God that, even though life can be so hard, I get to face it now with His help.

Our choices and actions always have consequences, and without accepting the redemption made available by Jesus' death in our place on that cross, we will be held accountable and judged for our choices and actions, ultimately facing eternal separation from God in eternity. (This eternal separation would actually be granting us what we ultimately made the choice for: an existence without God).

There is a verse in the Bible that says, "Like a dog that returns to his vomit is a fool who repeats his folly" (Proverbs 26:11 ESV). I didn't just return to the proverbial vomit; I bathed & relished in it. I am writing this for those who find themselves in a place of emptiness, darkness, or frustration. The well-worn saying of "sin will take you farther than you ever planned to go" is well-worn for a reason. No one intends to wreck their life or go so far, but the greatness of God is that it's never too late to escape. As long as you have breath, there is an amazing hope and help available.

Many people find what feels like true happiness in this short life on earth, living without Jesus. Ultimately though, there is right and there is wrong and there are consequences for our choices both ways. The Bible says, "There is a way that seems right to a man, but its end it is the way of death" (Proverbs 14:12 ESV). Jesus showed us the way for living and being right with God when He said, "I am the way, and the truth and the life. No one comes to the Father except through me" (John 14:6 ESV). That isn't a statement of exclusion, but an amazing inclusion—an invitation extended to every soul on this earth. He's not a cuddly, tidy, blushing Jesus that just wants to make you happy... He's Jesus Christ, Jehovah Jireh, Son of God, who is mighty to *save*! A strong, tough, rebel against the religious, who orders the universe, yet is aware of your every heartbeat. We are loved far more than you and I could ever comprehend.

We have no real control over life's circumstances, but ultimately life happens, we happen, and yet we have eternal spirits that will live forever. I have found peace and eternal purpose for my existence in Jesus alone, and I believe that none of us will ever truly be "fixed" or fulfilled until we get right with the One who created us. The same grace that saved me is available to you. I can only point to the Savior who loved me and died for my sins. I don't know your story, but He absolutely does. He changed my world and purpose. He gave me a new life, but not because of anything I ever did. It is everything *He* did. It is grace: pure, amazing, over-whelming grace, and I thank God for loving prodigals.

❦

Everyone Can be Changed

You've now had the opportunity to read two accounts of changed lives: first my story, and then, years later, my daughter's experience with transforming grace. Before we part company, I want to share two more things with you. Some time ago, I was sitting with a couple at a table in their home, talking about their family situation. They brought up the fact that they had a son who is not right with God. He had been on drugs, he had been in prison, and he had squandered multiple opportunities to change. The mother said to me, "He will never change. We have given up on him and have pretty much written him off." I couldn't believe my ears when she said that. We must remember God loves us so much, and *He* doesn't give up on us. If you have a friend or some family member who is in darkness and separated from God, never give up on them; keep praying for them until you see a spiritual breakthrough. God's mercy is end-less.

I read a story about a desperate mother who sought a pardon for her son from the first Emperor Napoleon of France. However, when she asked, the emperor said, "It was his second offense - justice demands his death." "I don't ask for justice," replied the mother, "I plead for mercy." But the emperor said, "He does not deserve mercy." "Sire!" cried the mother, "It would not be mercy if he deserved it, and mercy is all I ask for." "Well, then," said the emperor, "I will have mercy," and her son was saved. I tell you, God is infinitely more merciful than any emperor. If we pray for mercy and pardon for those we love, God will hear our prayers and He will move in their lives. Never ever give up on anyone. You are the lifeline to that soul that is sinking into darkness.

Yes, This Includes *You*

Finally, and most importantly, maybe you are not right with God, and you are in darkness. God wants to turn the light of eternal life on in your spirit. The Bible calls it being "born-again." It *is* a new birth, the doorway to a new life and a living, working relationship with none other than God Himself. It starts with receiving a full pardon for your past sinful life. John 3:16 (KJV) says, "For God so loved the world, that he gave his only begotten Son, that whosoever believeth in him should not perish, but have everlasting life." Jesus, God's only Son, paid for our sins with His own blood on the cross; the innocent, who did not deserve judgment, took all the punishment for the guilty. God did this out of love for us, when we were so lost when we could not help ourselves. The amazing reality is this: a full pardon for all sin is waiting for anyone who will accept it. It's like you're sitting in a jail cell, waiting for your sentence to be carried out, and that sentence is DEATH. First is physical death, followed by eternal death....forever. Then the jailer comes and unlocks your cell door. He opens it and says, "Your penalty has been paid by someone else - you're free to go." Would you just sit there? Or, would you get up and walk out of that cell with a brand-new lease on life? Even though pardon for sin is available, it must be received and activated. You need to stand up and walk out of that jail cell.

In 1830, a man named George Wilson was convicted of robbing the US Mail and was therefore sentenced to be hanged. President Andrew Jackson issued a pardon for Wilson, but he refused to accept it. The matter went to Chief Justice Marshall, who concluded that Wilson would have to be executed. "A pardon is a slip of paper," wrote Marshall, "the value of which is determined by the acceptance of the person to be pardoned. If it is refused, it is no pardon. George Wilson must be hanged."

Today, God wants to take you off death row. "For the wages of sin is death; but the gift of God is eternal life through Jesus Christ our Lord." (Romans 6:23 KJV). I urge you, in the next few moments, to take advantage of God's free gift. Accept His pardon, and the light will go on inside your spirit. In that moment, you will find that you have been born again to a new life. Your sins will be forgiven, guilt will lift off you, and you will feel peace on the inside. On top of that, you will have eternal life and you will not be judged. Jesus said, "Very truly I tell you, whoever hears my word and believes him who sent me has eternal life and will not be judged but has crossed over from death to life" (John 5:24 NIV).

I want to pray a prayer with you right now. It's the same prayer that I prayed many years ago that revolutionized my life. It asks for God's forgiveness and receives His pardon. It doesn't take a lot of words to activate something very powerful. The words "I do" take you to be my wedded husband, or my wedded wife, activate a lifelong covenant relationship of marriage. In the same way, the simple words of this prayer will activate a personal covenant relationship with God that will last forever. To pray that prayer, we must decide that we want to live the new life God has for us and decide to stop living the way we used to. If that is your heart - if you want to change - He will save you in these next few moments and give you spiritual power to live differently than you have in the past. If that is what's in your heart to do, pray this prayer with me, out loud if you can.

Prayer

Father God, I come to you in Jesus' name. Lord, I admit that I'm a sinner and I need Your grace. I believe You died on the cross for me and You rose again. I ask You into my heart. Forgive my sins and make me Your child. I receive Your grace. Thank You for saving me. I will follow You.

Congratulations! You have just entered into the guilt free zone, the peace zone, the love zone; you're a member of God's eternal family. As you read this, I pray to God to cancel every plan the devil has for your life right here and now:

God, I ask you to teach this new member of your family how to live a different life. Teach them how to walk in Your grace and let them not miss anything that You have planned for them. In Jesus' name. Amen.

I have one last promise from God's word for you. He is going to provide you with all the spiritual power you need to totally change and walk the new pathway you are on. John 1:12 (KJV) says, "But as many as received him, to them gave the power to become the sons of God, even to them that believe on his name."

God bless you in your new walk!

Carly's Notes

1. Regarding Depression: Years after receiving help for my depression, I came across a questionnaire on clinical depression. It asked 14 questions and said that if you answered "yes" to 5 or more and had experienced it for 2 weeks or more, that you had what would be deemed clinical depression. I answered positive for almost every single question, each of which had been true for years upon years. There are different aspects to the source of depression. Some is legitimate physical illness or chemical imbalance. Sometimes it is the results of emotional trauma, a spiritual issue, or just the natural ebb and flow of life as it cycles. Those who have never experienced the empty hell of true depression are quick to dismiss it as weakness or something imaginary that can be easily overcome if one really tried. Well-meaning as it may be, these sentiments are absolutely false and offer no hope or help to those who truly experience it. If you think you may be experiencing depression or know someone who might be, talk to your doctor, pastor, or counselor. I want to encourage you not to continue just existing in depression; there is help available.

2. Regarding Sexuality (and Other Matters of Discipline): Are we not more than our desires? My belief is that we are *more* than our desires. We are *more* than our inclinations. We are *more* than our preferences. To say that we must be and act on tendencies or inclinations we were born with is to cheapen the realization of what it is to be a spiritual being. While Christians are known for putting homosexuality on a pedestal of sin, isolating sexuality from other sin misses the point. Yes, sexuality is more encompassing and affects far more than just eating an extra cookie would, in that we are spiritual beings, not just physical. Yet sexuality is actually as much a discipline

as other inclinations, urges, temptations, and desires. A much greater discipline to be sure, but a discipline none-theless. Eating, drinking, anger, adultery, etc.: all are an issue of sin, but there is a self-control, empowered by a power *outside* of ourselves: The Holy Spirit. Aside from Him, we will always give in whether mentally/emotionally or in actual physical realization. Only a power outside of and greater than ourselves can enable us by other-worldly, supernatural strength. Super. Natural. In the nat-ural we will always fall to our natural born inclinations or be miserable in not fulfilling our temptations. *Super*natu-ral indicates something greater than the natural - what we, in and of ourselves, are capable of.

Take Away:

For some, being a Christian (a follower of Jesus) might feel like Carly's first trip to a foreign country. The words, music, and customs found in church and practiced by Christians may seem very strange and unfamiliar, and yet God's grace translates through it all. Jesus loves you, died for you, and wants to have a life-long relationship with you. Jesus wants us, and we desperately NEED Him! Carly pointed out that living life without God can seemingly be fun, exciting, and full of adventure. As we distract ourselves with our pursuits of happiness, fun, and adventure, we find that our pursuits are never enough - they're simply not fulfilling in ways that can last. The good news is, in all things and in all circumstances, Jesus Christ IS enough. While so many things in life are fleeting and temporary, God gives us this great promise in 1 Corinthians 13:13 (NIV):

> "And now these three remain: faith, hope, and love. But the greatest of these is love."

God loved us so much that he sacrificed His son, Jesus, so that we could be made whole and right before God. Our right standing with God isn't because of something we did or didn't do, but rather, it is only through what Jesus did for us by dying on the cross for our sins. We don't need to first understand the words, music, and customs of Christians - we simply need to be able to cry out to Jesus that we want Him in our life and that we believe in who He is and what He has done for us.

Discussion

1. When you think about church, Christians, or the Bible, does it at all seem strange or unfamiliar? Explain.

2. Do you see and understand your need of Jesus in your life? Why or why not?

3. How is knowing about and believing in Jesus different than entering into a personal and meaningful relationship with Jesus?

4. Have you, or are you ready to, start your relationship with Jesus?

Activate Your Faith

- To hear a little bit more about how to start your new walk with God, please watch my short eight-minute podcast Exit Strategy at http://rockfordres.org/media/exitstrategy/

- Memorize and ponder the following scripture verses:

  o *"For God so loved the world, that he gave his only begotten Son, that whosoever believeth in him should not perish, but have everlasting life"* (John 3:16 KJV).

  o *"Very truly I tell you, whoever hears my word and believes him who sent me has eternal life and will not be judged, but has crossed over from death to life"* (John 5:24 NIV).

  o *"For the wages of sin is death; but the gift of God is eternal life through Jesus Christ our Lord"* (Romans 6:23 KJV).

About the Author

DOUG BERGSMA. author of *The Dark Side of Faith – don't waste your pain,* serves as the Lead Pastor of Resurrection Life Church in Rockford, Michigan. He previously served as a worship leader, Bible teacher, and elder with Maranatha ministries in Grandville, Michigan for 20 years. Doug also attended Christ for the Nations Institute in Dallas, Texas. He is happily married to his wife Caryn, and is the proud father of four sons and two daughters. Over a period of time, Doug became connected with Resurrection Life Church in Grandville, Michigan under the leadership of Pastor Duane Vander Klok. During this period of time, he participated in missions, crusades overseas, and worship recording projects. In 2002, Doug and his wife Caryn were led to plant a church in Rockford, Michigan. Since then, the church has experienced vibrant, explosive growth. Doug's sermon podcasts and the church's well-known transformation videos (celebrating stories of changed lives) are being viewed throughout the region and across the country.